RECIPES OF MY 15 GRANDMOTHERS

Unique Recipes and Stories from the Times of the Crypto-Jews during the Spanish Inquisition

GENIE MILGROM

Merry Christmas 2020
To: Milton
From: Eloise
ENJOY!

gefen
publishing house
בית הוצאה לאור גפן
Est. 1981
JERUSALEM ◆ NEW YORK

Cover Photo: Ron Kriss, Susan Miguel and Luis Garcia-Mesa
Cover Design: Dragan Bilic
Typesetting: Optume Technologies

ISBN: 978-965-229-969-7
1 3 5 7 9 8 6 4 2

Gefen Publishing House Ltd.
6 Hatzvi Street
Jerusalem 9438614, Israel
972-2-538-0247
orders@gefenpublishing.com

Gefen Books
140 Fieldcrest Ave.
Edison NJ, 08837
516-593-1234
orders@gefenpublishing.com

www.gefenpublishing.com
Printed in Israel

Library of Congress Cataloging-in-Publication Data

Names: Milgrom, Genie, author.
Title: Recipes of my 15 grandmothers / Genie Milgrom.
Description: Jerusalem, Israel : Gefen Publishing House Ltd., [2019]
Identifiers: LCCN 2018061377 | ISBN 9789652299697
Subjects: LCSH: Jewish cooking. | Jews--Spain--History. | LCGFT: Cookbooks.
Classification: LCC TX724 .M53 2019 | DDC 641.5/676--dc23 LC record available at
    https://lccn.loc.gov/2018061377

This book is dedicated to my dad, George Medina. He was ninety-one when I lost him, and I realized that he had always been my number one cheerleader and the champion of all my projects. Dad stood by me as I went from being a Cuban Catholic young woman to a Jewish Orthodox woman. He never judged me and was always incredibly supportive. He was proud of me as I searched and found my Jewish ancestry, and he would have been so proud of me today as I come to publish this recipe book that speaks volumes of the legacy that was passed down to me. Thank you, Dad, for teaching me to reach for the moon and for making all my accomplishments possible. I miss you so much, but my life and successes are a tribute to your excellence.

Common Measurement Conversions

1 ounce = 28 g
1 pound = 450 g
1 cup (liquid) = 8 ounces = 240 ml
1 pint = 2 cups = ½ quart = ½ liter
1 quart = 4 cups = 1 liter
1 gallon = 4 quarts = 16 cups = 4 liters

Fahrenheit /Celsius
275°F = 135°C
300°F = 150°C
350°F = 175°C
375°F = 190°C
400°F = 200°C
450°F = 230°C

1 inch = 2.5 cm

The Test Cooks

Below is a list of friends and colleagues from around the world who took the time in their own kitchens to cook the centuries-old recipes of my grandmothers. They tweaked them with modern measurements and ingredients until they made them work! I will always be grateful to this amazing group of men and women for their invaluable contribution to the preservation of my family memories, using their hands and giving of their hearts.

Thank you so much!

Jackie Abels – United States – Frituras

Alfredo Alonso Estenoz – United States – Almond Sofrito

Jackie Attias – United States – Buñuelos del Viento

Rebbetzin Sima Becker – United States – Sponge Cake

Liliana Benveniste – Argentina – Huevos Moles

Esperanza Bonet Roig – Mallorca – Rosquitas

Corinne Brown – United States – Galleticas

Judith Cohen – Canada – Rosquitas

Patty East – United States – Pollo Dulce

Denise and Nya Febres Rodriguez – United States – Rosquillas

Skip Feinstein – United States – Mantecaditos

Cristina Lea Fernandes – United States – Chuletas Tia Paulita

Marcia Fine – United States – Mantecaditos

Su Fink – United States – Anise Cookies; Beet and Avocado Salad

Marcia Finkel – United States – Spanish Cake

Laura Garcia – United States – Bollo Maimon

Batya Goldman–United States – Torta de Manzana

Schulamith and Erga Halevy – Israel – Stuffed Eggplant

Kelsey Harlow – United States – Dulces en Almibar

Nicole Hernandez – United States – Tocino del Cielo

Jesus Jambrina – United States – Almond Sofrito

Nilza Karl – United States – Cocadas

Cindy Lewin – United States – Royal Butter Cake

Marsha Margulies – United States – Cocido Madrileño

Bini Masin – United States – Vegetable Soufflé

Mari Menda – Brazil – Chicken Empanada

Carl Montoya – United States – Pollo Fabiola; Beets with Oranges

Adina Moryosef – Israel – Sugar Cookies

Maji Pace Ramos – United States – Anise Bread

Eve Murphy Parente – United States – Carrot-Shaped Potatoes

Teri and Kristina Perez – United States – Dulces en Almibar

Marge Prenner – United States – Palitos del Cielo Tia Paulita

Kit Racette – Canada – Panatela

Jen Resnick – United States – Orejuelas y Pestiños

Sandi Samole – United States – Bollos de Leche

Donna Slotsky – United States – Fish Chowder

Yael Trusch–United States – Bizcochos

Lissette Valdes–Valle – United States – Buñuelos de Yuca

Liana Vega Hernandez– United States – Magdalenas

Fay Weinberg – United States – Almendrados

Helaine Weissman – United States – Sweet Toasts

Debbie Wohl–Isard – United States – Tortilla Española

Kim Wolfenzon – United States – Coconut Sweets in Syrup

Devorah Zachariah – United States – Chiricaya

Open Letters to My Grandmothers

To My Maternal Grandmother, Maneni

Dear Maneni, you were a grounded, stable, and loving grandmother who not only passed down my Jewish heritage to me in a myriad of indirect ways but also taught me about *tzedakah* (charity and giving to the poor), *bikur cholim* (visiting the sick), and *chesed* (kindness), in all your dealings. Maneni, I miss you, and I thank you for giving me back the ancestral memories of our family and my rich Jewish heritage. It changed my life and who I eventually became. In retrospect...there was so much that I would have asked you before you slipped away. I now have so many unanswered questions. I just wish I had known that you knew we were Jewish; maybe you could have spoken to me about it directly. I will always love you, and I miss you every single day of my life.

To My Paternal Grandmother, Mati

Mati, I thank you for showing me the quiet and gentle ways of strength. You were always the most religious in the family, and I admired that no matter where we were you never failed to pray, at the very least, an hour a day. I remember so well sleeping in your bed as a child and how you sat up for hours and even if you were tired, you always finished your prayers and taught me how to be grateful and to pray every single day. You were so close to G-d and it showed in all aspects of your life. Your open-door policy to family and people in need, and your incredible nature of helping everyone impacted me in so many positive ways. At the time, I saw that extended hand and willingness to cook meals for the sick as a normal way of life, yet as I became older I understood that it was what made you so special. Every time I open my home or extend my own hand to help, I know you are behind me and still guiding me. I always admired you and the legacy of my Costa Rican French lineage holds a special place in my heart. Thank you, Mati. I will forever hold you in my heart, and even after all these years since you left us, I still reach for the phone at least once a month seeking your gentle warmth. I miss you and thank you for teaching me how to be kind and loving at all times and to always judge others favorably.

Contents

Contents

Prologue

I was born in Havana, Cuba, to a Roman Catholic family of Spanish origins. I was raised in that religion and attended only Catholic schools from nursery school through college. I had no idea that deep inside I held an identity different from the one I had been born into. From a young age, I had always felt Jewish and had an affinity toward all things Jewish. Deep in my soul I knew that I was very different from my family members. This feeling grew stronger and stronger through the years until finally, in my thirties, I converted to Orthodox Judaism, leaving me to fend for myself as a single mom with two young children. It was much later that I started to fully research my own genealogy and found an unbroken maternal lineage going back twenty-two generations to 1405 pre-Inquisition Spain and Portugal. The knowledge that my family was always Jewish turned my life upside down.

As I headed back in time, and after all the rigorous paperwork had been done and recorded, I realized that I was more interested in personal details about my own family, such as what they did for a living or how they moved from village to village while being persecuted, than just the thousands of names on legal and religious documents. I began to study the back story of the many names on the genealogy charts and learned that in the 1500s my family had been heavily engaged in the guild trades, with occupations such as shoemaker, furrier, tanner, and even butcher. These were all occupations that were known to be those of the Crypto-Jewish population at the time, as not all lines of work were open to them. I also learned that in the 1700s and 1800s my family had been in the wine business as either owners of vineyards, winegrowers, or wine merchants. The late 1800s and 1900s came, and the new family businesses were mostly in haberdashery. They sold buttons, ribbons, and lace, and it was with this trade that they left Spain and migrated to all parts of the Caribbean and South America. They opened small haberdashery shops in Argentina and Chile. In Cuba, my family started small in the haberdashery business and eventually opened large silk-stocking manufacturing plants. Finally, in the United States, they owned factories in Miami producing silk screen clothing for men and women.

As I was reading through the files about their diaspora, I realized that most of the documents made mention only of the men. I learned through the last wills and testaments all about their work and travel, but for the most part, there was a total silence about the women. The women were mentioned mostly in the last wills and testaments as the heirs to their husbands. Little by little, as the family business in Spain shifted, when they moved into haberdashery, the women started to be more prevalent in the archival records.

I know for a fact that my family was Jewish in the late 1400s and Crypto-Jewish after that, as they hid underground and practiced the Jewish faith while pretending to be Catholic. I have the Inquisition court cases for over forty of my relatives that sit squarely on my maternal lineage. I learned that on my mother's side, they passed through the Inquisitions of Sevilla, Coimbra, and Evora, while to a lesser degree, from my father's side, a handful passed through the Inquisitions of Cadiz and the Canary Islands.

As I was growing up, my grandmother Maneni transmitted some of her Jewish ancestral memories to me. She never once mentioned that there was a Jewish connection but rather taught them to me as "family traditions." She had five grandchildren and was very close to all of them, yet she only chose to pass these memories down to me. She must have seen in me the potential to soak up the information and use it in my own life for transmittal to future generations of women. Most of these traditions were passed down to me during the times that we cooked together in her small kitchen in Miami.

She taught me to always check for spots of blood in eggs and never to just put them into a mixing bowl with other ingredients before placing them in a cup and inspecting them individually beforehand. She told me that if even one spot was present, we would have to throw away the egg, as we could not use it for cooking. My grandmother also taught me to wash all produce well before using any vegetable, and to separate the leaves of lettuce and other greens and wash them individually as well. I did not understand this because she made a delicious soup that used a lot of Swiss chard which would be boiled for a long time, but she insisted that the greens be inspected carefully before being put into the boiling pot. I was taught to always rinse rice twice in case there were any insects. This meticulous checking and rechecking for insects is still done today in countless homes that keep the strict kosher laws.

Throughout this book, there are other Jewish customs that were also passed down to me while cooking in her tiny kitchen. Many of these customs are Jewish dietary laws, although I did not know it at the time, as they were passed down as merely "family customs." Eggs are always checked for any spot of blood, as it is forbidden to consume even a drop of blood in Jewish law. The custom of cracking the egg into a cup before putting it into a recipe is still practiced today by kosher cooks around the world. Checking the individual leaves of all vegetables is also part of the laws of kashrut. Before any vegetable is used, it is not only washed thoroughly, but leaves are taken apart and visually inspected for insects, as we are forbidden to eat insects. Perhaps the knowledge of the *why* of these customs did not persist through the centuries in my family, but it is incredible that the actual kosher traditions did.

I returned to Judaism when I was in my thirties. It was a very difficult transition, as my family remained Catholic. I came alone to the religion of my ancestors and for several years lost most of my friends from my previous life and had a difficult time fitting in to my new life, but I persisted because I knew it was the correct place for me to be from a spiritual point of view. Naturally, my mom was not happy about this. I asked her often if she had any documentation or paperwork from past times. She told me again and again that she did not have anything that had been passed down from previous generations. All of the paperwork and documentation that I had amassed to prove my Jewish lineage was obtained from archives in Cuba, and then Spain and Portugal. I was unable to piece together anything from my family through paperwork that my mom may have kept. I understand her reticence now, but it was hard at the time because I had to claw my way through to gain any family information. I know now that my mom must have acted out of the fear that science tells us may come from genetic memory. Therefore, as hard as it was to do this work from scratch, there is a certain sense of accomplishment in knowing that I walked the road the hard way back to my past.

Finally, the sad day came when my mom could no longer live in her home, and it was at that moment that I found many old books full of pages of handwritten recipes and scraps of paper with small writing and tiny notes written in light pencil. All of these pages were done in different handwritings, some with more flourishes than others, but always written by the women. With this, I found the recipes of the grandmothers. I so appreciate that these hand-bound memories were never thrown away and I am able to share them with you today. I have to thank my mom for that because she knew that one day I would find them. She took the trouble to bring them from Spain to Cuba, and to pack them up and move them from house to house as we moved around in Miami and then Georgia and back to Miami. She did not give them over when I asked, but she also did not throw them away. The treasure trove I found that day was not only about recipes. It also included family trees, baby books, birth and death certificates, and the originals of what I had found in the archives. It corroborated a large chunk of information that I had found on my own.

Since my family was openly Catholic for over five hundred years, some of the recipes they recorded did not conform to the kosher laws. I have only included in this book those recipes that meet the kosher guidelines and that have also been modified and tested with the meats and products available to us today. An interesting point to note is that at no time, in all the hundreds of recipes, was there one that mixed meat and milk. Perhaps the memory of not eating certain types of meats was erased, but the separation of meat and milk continued through the centuries. In the kosher dietary laws, meat and milk are never used together in a recipe and also never mixed on the same plate. This separation is one of the strictest of the kosher laws. I also found recipes that could clearly be used for Passover which contained no flour and used potato starch instead. Sephardic Jews also used cornstarch instead of flour, and that is also prevalent in some recipes.

Sephardic and Ashkenazic foods are very different from each other and vary greatly from the foods the Spaniards brought out of Spain. However, there are many basic recipes of Spanish foods that were incorporated into the Sephardic recipes. When the Jews left Spain and settled primarily in the Ottoman Empire, they immediately blended in with the Muslims living in those lands. The flavors became more exotic, and the rich foods became even richer. The sugar-nuts-and-fruit desserts from Spain became even more flavorful – if that is possible – and the oil-rich and fried foods continued with new ingredients. The rise of the Sephardic foods leaves many to think that the Spanish Crypto-Jews ate in the same way, but this is not the case. Spanish food as it was passed down to us is heavy in tomato sauces, olives, sugar, flour, and oil. Spain and Portugal did not have access to all the delicacies that were available in the Ottoman Empire, making a clear distinction in our foods. Ashkenazic Jewish food is replete with flavors of their regions – mainly Germany, France, Poland, Russia, Lithuania, and Hungary – such as beets, chicken, potatoes, simple fish, noodles, pickled food, and stews, and are oftentimes considered to have originated from peasant food. This food was historically hardy, given the geographical location and the many cold winter months.

My sincere wish as I write this book is that my grandmothers will be proud of me for having given them their voices back via the written word. Through the centuries as the grandmothers moved from Braganza, Portugal, to Fermoselle, Spain, to Madrid, to the Canary Islands, on to Cuba, Costa Rica, and then to Miami, these cookbooks and loose papers that I now cherish were always with them. I have a huge box full of these notes and papers and bound books, and it is incredible that when they packed their belongings and moved their families to new villages or even across the oceans, these recipes were traveling with them as their most cherished possessions. I have brought the grandmothers back out into the open to proudly proclaim that they were Jewish. The Inquisition silenced many families, yet I was blessed to have been able to find my way back to Judaism and stand proudly among the Jewish People. I give honor to my grandmothers today. All twenty-two of them.

Introduction

As I embarked on this project, I gathered all the books and snippets of paper and sat the jumbled mass next to my computer. I must be honest and say that for a while I felt daunted. The stack of books and the tiny papers inside were staring me down, and I stared back. If I had been able to find my lineage after five hundred years then *surely,* I would be able to transcribe centuries-old recipes. The handwriting was light and faint, and at times, there were splatters and cross-outs that didn't make sense. But slowly I translated them from Spanish to English, and then I started changing the measurements to fit our standardized ones and the US measuring system. The recipes would call for 50 grams of sugar, and I would change to tablespoons and cups and so on. The bigger challenge came when the grandmothers would write things like "add a small goblet of water" or "an eggful of oil." I had to guess and estimate what they really meant.

The other challenge was to make sure that all the ingredients that I would exchange would be kosher, and to try to make some of the recipes pareve instead of dairy so that they would be more useful to the average kosher household. I also found that the ingredients used were mostly those from the western region of Spain where they lived, for example, olive oil, almonds, and anise. I held so many of these recipes in my hands and studied them so intently that it became possible for me to know if the recipe was from Spain, Portugal, Cuba, or even Costa Rica. The ingredients were usually a big giveaway. I have always felt blessed to have been able to travel in their footsteps, but so much more so now that I've held in my hands the very papers that they did when they brought the foods to their everyday and holiday tables.

Finally, when I had transcribed a large number of recipes, I suddenly realized that I would have to cook each one! *That* was what daunted me the most. I knew I needed a lot of help, and I turned to my friends – not only the women that I see on a continuous basis, but men and women I had met at conferences, some with Crypto-Jewish backgrounds and others who are academics in this field. I contacted my colleagues – musicians, authors, and professors – and before I knew it, I had more women offering to make the recipes than recipes typed up. I am eternally grateful to all my friends who came out again and again to help without my asking.

I was handpicking each recipe to match the person I was giving it to, and in this book, I cover not only the history of the recipe in the context of the Crypto-Jewish phenomenon, but also, I talk about the person who volunteered to make it. I find it is important to showcase these men and women who many times were born into the same type of background as me. I always try to teach and talk about our history, and I felt that this would be a great way to do it, via the foods. I did receive a lot of questions about the use of kosher meats back in the day and how some of these recipes survived not only generations, but centuries.

As the process of trying out the recipes progressed, I started getting emails and calls telling me that most of the time, the dessert recipes tasted too "eggy." I also heard that the recipes were not working because they were too "soupy." Some of my friends had to make the recipes three or four times to get them to work, each time cutting down the amount and size of eggs, again and again until it was perfect. We have no idea what size eggs were used by the grandmothers, but one thing we know for sure is that they were very small. The other comments were that they tasted too much like olive oil, which, as you will see, is the oil that is used the most. My family, being from a region that grows olives, probably used even more than usual, and it would have been the very best and tastiest oil, which naturally doesn't fit well in a dessert recipe and much less a cookie. I left in the olive oil in most recipes to stay true to history, but many of the cooks did change it.

Our first big reveal came during a Friday night Sabbath meal in my home with a very close group of friends who had each made one of the recipes. I was so excited to host a Shabbat meal dedicated to the grandmothers. I personally made five or six meat recipes, and each of my friends had prepared a different dish. I cautioned my close-knit group of Ashkenazic friends that it would be a special and different night without their traditional Sabbath foods such as gefilte fish and matzah ball soup. What would be served that evening would be over the top and very different.

We started with the garbanzo empanadas, which were excellent, and we ate them with hummus. We continued with the hornazo, which I highly recommend, followed by the cocido madrileño and many other meat-filled delicacies. There was a beet and avocado salad and then a table full of artisanal-looking cookies and cakes. It was very different, and throughout the meal we recounted stories of how the Crypto-Jews had eaten and preserved their traditions. It was a rich and fun night of sharing, and I thank my good friends Jackie Abels, Su Fink, Nilza Karl, Marsha Margulies, and Fay Weinberg for all their help and encouragement along the way. I especially want to thank Nilza, who attempted the cocada recipe at least six times before getting the perfect and exact proportion of eggs to sugar! We not only had an amazing and fun night, but I was also able to ascertain that the recipes did work, albeit with a lot of tweaking.

As time has progressed and I have rewritten even *more* recipes, I have noticed a clear lack of fresh vegetables and fruit. I still cannot understand why there are so few recipes with fresh ingredients and almost none with fruit, but I am told that these were usually eaten fresh and not cooked into recipes as we do today.

Each recipe I will give over has a bit of history attached as well as some background on the women who helped me make this historical work happen. I could not have done it without them.

In the book, I have added a label to each recipe indicating its level of difficulty. All of the recipes are able to be cooked in a kosher kitchen and using kosher products. I checked each and every one of the ingredients and found they were available kosher if desired. I also labeled each one to be either dairy, meat, or pareve, and if applicable suitable for Passover or easily modifiable for Passover use. I will be listing recipes in alphabetical order within their category, but I wish to start with the most meaningful recipe that was passed down to me, and that is periquillos. Enjoy!

Periquillos

Description: A typical fried dough with layers of anise and other flavors
Level: Difficult
Kosher: Pareve

Life growing up in a traditional Cuban Catholic household was replete with grand celebrations every year, with all the family and cousins running around, ripping brightly colored paper from the many presents that were exchanged. Those years would not have been complete without multiple colorful tins that my grandmother had filled with a sweet recipe from Fermoselle, Spain, the village of my ancestors. This periquillo recipe was first taught to me when I was a little girl of about ten. My grandmother always told me that I had to make it with her to be able to master it. She taught me that cooking is not just about reading, and that when you make a recipe it is important to have the recipe become a part of you. It was from this periquillo recipe and the large amounts of dough she would use as she doubled and tripled the measurements that she taught me the ancient Jewish law of taking a little bit of the dough, wrapping it tight (we use aluminum foil), and throwing it in the back of the oven to be burned – she said it was for "good luck." I had no idea then that the information would be crucial as I grew into an observant Jewish woman and that the act of separating the dough comes with this blessing that all Orthodox women make when "taking challah" (*hafrashat challah* in Hebrew).

Baruch Atah Adoshem Elokeinu Melech Ha'Olam asher kiddeshanu b'mitzvotav v'tzivanu l'hafrish challah (min ha'isah).
Blessed are You, Lord, our G-d, King of the universe, Who has sanctified us with His commandments and commanded us to separate challah (from the dough).

I never learned the blessing from my grandmother, as such overt Jewish memories were never passed down to me, but the subtle memory – the act of actually putting the dough in aluminum foil and burning it – was conveyed to me year after year as we made these fried ancestral delicacies. The last time we made these together, she was getting tired very often and could no longer stand for long periods. I vividly recall as she sat at her little round, white glass table in her kitchen and directed me from there. That last year I forgot to put the dough in the aluminum, and she was so visibly upset at me. Looking back, I am certain she knew it was her last time, and if I would forget to put the dough in the oven while she lived, how much more would I forget after she was gone.

Her name was Ascension, which is a very Catholic name, and her friends called her Nena. I called her Maneni. I honor her memory today by telling her in this book that I never forgot to put the dough in aluminum and I also never forgot a word she taught me. I have taught her granddaughters and great-granddaughters to never forget as well.

This family recipe actually belongs to the whole village of Fermoselle in Spain. No other town has claimed this special recipe. In the village of Fermoselle they tell me that the periquillo recipe is centuries old and was only eaten during the festive Spanish Carnival season in February and March.

In Spanish, a *perico* is a parrot, and when fried, these delicacies open up and look like a parrot beak. I make these once or twice a year, and I always give them out to the family in tins as Maneni used to. It was not necessary to give this recipe over to someone else to cook because I tweaked it through the years as I made them in that tiny kitchen, standing for hours side by side with her. I miss her so much, and when I make the periquillos in my own kitchen, it is always with a range of emotions from happiness to sadness. It is interesting to note that many happy Jewish traditions are laced with some sadness, such as the breaking of the glass under the wedding canopy in a Jewish wedding.

Periquillos

6 large eggs
28 rounded tablespoons or 3½ cups sugar
¾ cup olive oil
6 tablespoons anise liqueur
2 (1-ounce) bottles anise essence

5½ cups flour, plus 1 cup (what this means is that you start with 5½ cups and try to form the periquillo balls, continuing to add flour as necessary up to 1 cup more for a total of maximum 6½ cups)
Oil for frying

Mix the eggs well with the sugar until the sugar is dissolved. I have always mixed this by hand. Add the oil, liqueur, and anise essence, and mix well. Add the flour slowly by incorporating the first 5½ cups until you can start molding small balls with your hands. Your hands need to be clean and coated with olive oil as you form the periquillos. The balls should be about the size of a ping-pong ball or a bit smaller. You only add enough flour to make small, 1 to 1½-inch-wide balls. Keep your hands well oiled to make it easier to form the balls. If there is more flour in the recipe than needed, they will be too hard.

Heat the oil and drop the balls in one by one. Deep-fry until they are golden brown and a small "beak" opens up. Place on paper towels to drain.

Makes about 40 small periquillos. They should be kept in tins to stay crispy. If you cover them with aluminum or plastic, they will get soggy.

Chicken Dishes

Baked Chicken Ajiaco

Description: A type of stew made in many Latin American countries
Level: Difficult
Kosher: Meat
Passover: Yes

My mom used to make this family recipe often. It is a dish that contains all the same ingredients as the stove-top ajiaco stew, but this one is baked in the oven. Ajiaco is made in many Latin American countries, and each recipe has subtle yet important variations that make it unique to each region. This particular recipe has a few "new world" ingredients, but the layers of flavor signal the old country! Quite a hit in our home every single time. There is another recipe in this book for a beef ajiaco which calls for many more ingredients. Although chicken ajiaco is widely known in Colombia, this one has the Cuban ingredients and a great comfort-food taste for me. Even though this recipe is ingredient heavy, all are common spices and vegetables, making it easier to just make at any time without special shopping. For Passover, you can easily leave out the corn if your tradition is not to eat corn during Passover.

½ cup olive oil

2 large white onions, peeled and cut in thick slices

5 cloves garlic, smashed

¼ cup small-chopped green peppers

1 (3-pound) chicken, cut into small cubes

Garlic powder

½ cup small-chopped onions

4 medium-sized Yukon Gold or similar potatoes, peeled and cut into thick slices

2 white sweet potatoes, peeled and cut into thick slices

2 whole fresh ears of corn, cut into halves

3 tablespoons tarragon flakes

¼ cup sliced garlic

2 cups red cooking wine

2 cups water

½ cup lemon juice

1 teaspoon salt

½ teaspoon pepper

Put the oil in a large pan and add the white onions, garlic, and green peppers. Cook this "sofrito" until the onions are transparent. Coat the chicken in garlic powder and toss until browned in the sofrito mixture.

Layer the chopped onions, potatoes, sweet potatoes, corn, tarragon, and garlic cloves in a baking dish. Add the wine, water, lemon juice, and salt and pepper. Place the browned chicken pieces on top, cover tightly with aluminum foil, and place in oven. Bake for 1½ hours and serve over rice or with vegetables.

Chicken Empanada

Description: A pastry filled with chicken
Level: Difficult
Kosher: Meat

Mari Menda, a journalist from Sao Paulo, Brazil, tested this recipe in her kitchen. I had contacted her brother Nelson Menda, a Brazilian journalist living in Miami, and who, some time ago, had written an article about my work with Crypto-Jewry when I wrote my book *My 15 Grandmothers*. When he heard about the ongoing project of the recipe book, he enlisted his sister Mari, who has been a great help. Mari made the recipe and loved it. Her changes and tweaks are below. Thank you to the Menda family! Mari recently offered to cook for us any time we needed new recipes. So appreciative of you, Mari.

Dough

2 cups all-purpose flour, divided into 2
1 teaspoon salt
1½ teaspoons baking powder

1 cup shortening
1 cup pareve milk, unflavored
2 tablespoons sugar
2 medium eggs, beaten

Mix together all the ingredients except the eggs, by hand, until well blended, using only 1 of the 2 cups of flour. Add the eggs and blend in until all are well mixed. Cover with a damp cloth and set bowl in a warm place for 15 to 20 minutes. Mix in the second cup of flour little by little until you can separate the dough easily from the bottom of the bowl.

Filling

1 onion, finely chopped

Olive oil, enough for sautéing

1½ cups shredded cooked chicken (for the wet part of the filling)

2 tomatoes, peeled and chopped

1 cup chicken broth

1 egg yolk

Salt and pepper

Meats to set aside till you build the empanada:

— ¼ pound assorted cold cuts or deli meats

— 1 cup shredded cooked chicken (in addition to the chicken for the wet part of the filling)

— ½ pound veal or beef sausages, cut in half lengthwise, or other meats of your choice

Egg white, whipped, for egg wash at end

Sauté the onion in olive oil. Add the 1½ cups chicken, tomatoes, chicken broth, and egg yolk, and mix until well blended. Sauté a few minutes until cooked through. Add salt and pepper to taste and set aside until you build your empanada.

Empanada

Lay out the dough on a floured surface and cut in half. Roll out to make 2 squares about 10 to 12 inches square each, and cover 1 square with sliced cold cuts or deli meats, the 1 cup shredded chicken, sausages, and other meats you may have chosen. Add the sautéed chicken filling on top of the sliced deli meats to make the dish moist. If you skip this step of the wet chicken filling, the empanada will be way too dry. Place the other square on top and seal with your fingers. Poke holes with a fork on top of the pastry to prevent it from growing too tall and breaking open. Brush with egg white and bake at 350° for 45 minutes until golden brown.

Chicken Fricassee

Description: A typical Spanish chicken dish
Level: Difficult
Kosher: Meat
Passover: Modifiable

This is a typical recipe of most of the Caribbean. It is made often in Cuba and Puerto Rico, and you can find variations in the Dominican Republic as well as in Jamaica. In the Spanish-speaking islands, it is known as fricassee de pollo. In Jamaica, the only difference is that there would be a heavy dose of hot sauce or hot chili peppers added. This is one of the best chicken dishes, and I have made it many a time. The exotic blend of flavors is incredible. It is actually a go-to recipe for me, and I highly recommend it.

1 cup olive oil
2 large white onions, peeled and
  cut into small pieces
2 green peppers, cut into small pieces
12 tomatoes, cut into small pieces
1 (3-pound) chicken, cut up,
  preferably with skin removed
2 cups water
1 teaspoon salt
$1/8$ teaspoon pepper
1 pound russet potatoes, peeled and
  cut into cubes
2 large apples, peeled and cut into cubes

1 cup dry white wine
Juice of two lemons
½ cup dark raisins
$1/3$ cup capers
¾ cup green olives
½ cup sweet green peas (can be
  frozen, but preferably canned)
½ cup sweet red pimentos, cut into
  small dice
3 tablespoons dry bread crumbs
6 slices toasted bread, cut into
  triangles

Put the oil in a large pan and add the onions, green pepper, and tomatoes. Cook this "sofrito" together until the onions are transparent. Add the chicken, making sure it is very dry.

Add the water, salt, pepper, and potatoes. Mix well and bring to a boil. Cover and simmer on medium heat for 30 minutes. Uncover and add the apples, wine, lemon juice, raisins, capers, olives, peas, and half of the pimentos. Cover again, bring to a boil, and cook on medium heat until the chicken is soft. Add the bread crumbs to thicken the sauce and take off the stove. Let it rest for 5 minutes and serve decorated with the rest of the red pimentos and the toast triangles.

Chicken in Almond Sauce

Description: A unique chicken dish with almonds
Level: Difficult
Kosher: Meat
Passover: Yes

A recipe using almonds. The village of my ancestors, Fermoselle, where they lived for 523 years, has huge vineyards, almond trees, and the finest olive trees, whose olives produce the purest of olive oils. Most of the recipes that were passed down contain one or more of these ingredients, and this one is no different. This delicious chicken with its blend of flavors is very indicative of that region in Spain. A true gem of a recipe!

1 (3-pound) chicken, cut into
    quarters
¼ pound margarine
Salt and pepper
Juice of 2 lemons

1 pound slivered almonds, lightly
    toasted in a frying pan
3 onions, peeled and cut small
2 tablespoons olive oil
1½ cups chicken broth
4 egg yolks

Wash and dry the chicken and rub well with half the margarine. Dust with salt, pepper, and the juice of 1 lemon. Place on a cookie sheet and bake in oven, uncovered, at 375°F approximately 45 minutes or until golden brown. While the chicken is cooking, start making the sauce. Grind the almonds finely in a food processor. Sauté the onions and almonds in the rest of the margarine and olive oil until the onions are transparent. Strain the mixture to keep out all the liquid. Beat the egg yolks by hand, and slowly add the onion and almond mixture. Mix well. Add the chicken broth and cook slowly over a low heat until it blends together, but don't let the eggs curdle. Preferably use a water bath, made by setting the pan inside another pan that has about an inch of water at the bottom. Serve hot over the chicken.

Chicken Salad

Description: A light and fun variation on chicken salad
Level: Easy
Kosher: Meat
Passover: Yes

This is a recipe that graced the tables of any "ladies'" gathering that my mother or both my grandmothers ever made. I can't recall a party that did not come along with the family chicken salad. It is a tried-and-true, incredibly good recipe. The secret is to cut the chicken finely and to keep the amount of mayonnaise as low as possible. I have also made this for parties and for picnics, and not only do memories of festivities from other times come flooding back, but the wholesome taste of this chicken salad comes through each and every time.

1 (3-pound) chicken or the equivalent in chicken breasts, cooked, skinned, and boned, and cut into small cubes
2 large eggs, hard-boiled
2 medium-sized red apples
1 cup chopped celery stalk
¼ cup finely chopped red pimentos
2 pounds russet potatoes, cooked and cut into small cubes
4–6 tablespoons mayonnaise or olive oil
½ cup sweet peas

Add all the ingredients to the chicken, except the mayonnaise or oil and the peas, and mix until well blended.

Add the mayonnaise or oil until thoroughly mixed and place in a crystal bowl. Decorate with the peas as desired.

Chicken Sofrito

Description: A savory chicken dish in an onion and green pepper base
Level: Medium
Kosher: Meat
Passover: Yes

6 chicken thighs with skin and bone
1 yellow onion, finely chopped
½ green pepper, finely chopped
Olive oil for sautéing
4 tablespoons dark raisins

6 large olives, crushed and cut into
    quarters
1 tablespoon sugar
1 tablespoon garlic powder

Boil the chicken thighs until the meat is cooked. Remove all skin and bones, and break up the chicken with your hands (do not chop with a knife). Set aside.

Sauté the onion and green pepper at medium-to-high heat in olive oil until the onion is transparent. This Spanish cooking mixture is one of several variations called sofrito.

Add the chicken, raisins, olives, sugar, and garlic powder into the sofrito mixture and simmer over low-to-medium heat for 25 minutes.

Pollo Dulce

Description: A sweet and fruity chicken dish
Level: Medium
Kosher: Meat
Passover: Modifiable

I recall eating this recipe one time only, when I was young. My mom had made it and told me that it was the recipe of her grandmother. We will never know how many generations back it was made, as how all these recipes came into my hands so late in life is still a mystery to me. I was happy that my old college roommate and BFF Patty East jumped at the chance to help out with this project. Patty has always been my cheerleader and supportive of all my projects since we were fifteen. She lives now in Dallas, and I don't see her as often as I would like, but I love that she came through for me yet again. She made the recipe and served it over rice. She did make a couple of modifications that are reflected below. Thank you, Patty!

1 whole chicken (3 to 5 pounds),
    cut into eighths
1 cup sweet wine
1 cup sugar
¼ pound margarine
1 teaspoon salt
¼ teaspoon pepper

½ teaspoon nutmeg
1 cup orange juice
¼ pound unsalted whole almonds,
    blanched
1 pound grapes, peeled
½ cup red maraschino cherries
2 tablespoons flour

Wash and dry the chicken thoroughly. Heat the wine in a Dutch oven on medium–high heat and then stir in the sugar until dissolved. Add the margarine to this liquid and slowly stir until all ingredients are dissolved and blended. Once the sauce is smooth, add the chicken and turn every few minutes from side to side to be sure it is fully coated. Let it boil a few minutes while turning it. Add the salt, pepper, and nutmeg, and mix together. Mix in the orange juice, almonds, grapes, and cherries. Cover the pot and cook for 2 hours until the chicken is done. Take some broth from the pot and place in a cup. Mix in the flour, adding additional broth so it won't lump. Pour this into the pot and continue to cook for 20 to 30 minutes to thicken. The recipe can be served over rice or vegetables.

Chicken with Onions

Description: A chicken dish loaded with unique flavors
Level: Easy
Kosher: Meat
Passover: Yes

This recipe, handed down from my grandmother Mati, is a one-pan, delicious chicken that can be made easily. The ingredients are the typical flavorful ones used in Caribbean cooking. It would be difficult to find a recipe that doesn't include sour oranges or bay leaf. This is so versatile, it can be made anytime and with minimal effort. Marinate the night before, and the next day you are ready to go with this. Just add rice and a vegetable side dish.

1 chicken, cut up
3 cloves garlic
¼ cup parsley
Juice of 6 sour oranges or lemons
Olive oil
12 small onions, peeled

12 small red potatoes with skin on
1 cup dry red wine
1 bay leaf
2 cloves garlic, smashed and diced
Salt and pepper

Marinate the chicken overnight with the garlic, parsley, and half the juice. Brown the chicken in a large saucepan in a little bit of olive oil. Place in a Dutch oven with the onions and potatoes. Add the wine, bay leaf, the rest of the juice, diced garlic, and salt and pepper to taste. Do not add water! Cover and simmer for 50 minutes. Remove the 3 whole garlic cloves. Serve over vegetables and rice or roasted potatoes.

Pollo Fabiola

Description: A roasted chicken delicacy
Level: Difficult
Kosher: Meat
Passover: Yes

I gave this recipe to Carl Montoya. Carl is from a similar background to mine and was happy to help out. I have known him for many years, and he is one active fellow in his community. I truly appreciate that he took the time to help out on this project. He made the chicken following all the directions, and some of his changes are listed below. He said the chicken was juicy but could have used a little more flavoring, which is why we added the onion powder. I think I would add some garlic powder as well. He told me it took him 2 hours from start to finish. I really appreciate this, Carl!

1 whole chicken
8 cloves garlic, peeled
1 onion, cut into quarters
Onion salt or onion powder (I would use just a little onion salt and be liberal with the onion powder, as kosher chickens are very salty)
1 cup white wine
¼ cup margarine, melted, or olive oil

Place the onion and garlic inside the chicken.

Sprinkle onion salt over the chicken. Pour wine and margarine over chicken and marinate for 2 hours, covered, in the refrigerator.

Cover the chicken with aluminum and bake at 350°F, allowing 20 minutes per pound of chicken. Carl suggests removing the foil from the chicken for the last 20 minutes so it will brown. The grandmothers had written down to broil for 20 minutes, and though Carl did just that, he feels it was not required as it browned quite nicely without.

Sofrito De Pollo

Description: A typical dish with a mix of sweet and salty flavors
Level: Medium
Kosher: Meat
Passover: Yes

This recipe is as much of a staple in Cuban cuisine as the picadillo recipe that appears later, in the meat section. It can be used inside empanadas, over white rice, or baked inside a pie shell (the pie is called a pastel de pollo). My grandmothers always had an extra pastel de pollo lying around when I would visit. It looked like a regular pie but had this yummy chicken filling inside. It was always served cold at parties and was such a great addition to the table. Those grandmothers were so smart!

6 chicken thighs with skin and bone
1 yellow onion, finely chopped
½ green pepper, finely chopped
Olive oil for sautéing
4 tablespoons dark raisins

6 large olives, crushed and cut into
    quarters
1 tablespoon sugar
1 tablespoon garlic powder

Boil the chicken thighs in water or a broth until the meat is cooked. Set aside and remove all skin and bones and break up the chicken with your hands (do not chop with a knife).

Sauté the onion and green pepper at medium-to-high heat in olive oil until the onion is transparent. Yet another variation on the Spanish cooking mixture called sofrito!

Add the chicken, raisins, olives, sugar, and garlic powder into the sofrito mixture and simmer over low-to-medium heat for 25 minutes.

Can be used inside empanadas, over white rice, or baked inside a covered pie shell. Drain well if using in a pie, and leave with all the liquids if serving over rice.

Meat Dishes

Ajiaco

Description: A hearty meat stew
Level: Difficult
Kosher: Meat
Passover: Yes

I know this dish comes from Cuba. I'm not sure from what years, but given the sheer amount of ingredients, I feel it was from an earlier time. Ajiaco is a dish eaten in two or three countries in South America as well as in Cuba. The Cuban version is very different, as it is made to be a stew with all the original products that are grown in Cuba, such as the yuca, malanga, green and sweet plantains, and sweet white potatoes. These products can be found in most major cities but also in smaller Cuban or Central American grocery stores. The ingredient list truly sounds like a checklist of all the products grown in Cuba. I have made this and used smaller amounts of all the ingredients because it seemed to be too many pounds of meat and other ingredients, and I was making it for a small group. I mostly left the amounts of the original ingredients to be as authentic as possible, but I did cut down on the amount of a couple of the meats. I suggest starting with a *very* large pot. This dish is not only hearty but also has a blend of flavors, and because of the way it is cooked, the flavors are layered. This dish can be easily made during Passover. If you don't eat corn during Passover, then simply leave it out and the ajiaco will still be wonderful.

16 cups water (4 quarts or 1 gallon)

½ pound beef chunks

½ pound lamb chunks

¼ pound skirt steak, soaked and separated

¼ pound yuca, peeled and cut into chunks

½ pound malanga (like taro), peeled and cut into chunks

¼ pound white sweet potato, peeled and cut into chunks

¼ pound regular sweet potato, peeled and cut into chunks

¼ pound regular potatoes, peeled and cut into chunks

4 fresh ears corn, peeled and cut into 2-inch rounds

2 green plantains, peeled and cut in rounds

2 sweet plantains, peeled and cut into rounds

Juice of 1–2 lemons

1 onion, cut into small pieces

1 green pepper, cut up small

3 cloves garlic, cut up small

6 tomatoes, cut into small pieces

½ cup olive oil

1½ teaspoons salt

¼ teaspoon pepper

Put water in a large soup pot and add the meats. Bring to a rolling boil, cover, and cook on medium heat for 40 minutes. Add the yuca, malanga, the 3 types of potato, and corn. Bring to the boil and cook, covered, another 30 minutes on medium heat. Add the green and sweet plantains and the juice of 1 lemon and cook for another 10 minutes. Make a sofrito by sautéing the onions, green pepper, garlic, and tomatoes in the olive oil, along with the salt and pepper. Add to mixture and boil for 5 minutes, then simmer for 10 more minutes. Add the juice of the second lemon if desired. I usually leave the second lemon out, but many say that the second lemon takes this recipe over the top. Serve hot.

Bola Catalana

Description: A specialty ground beef log from the Catalonia area of Spain
Level: Medium
Kosher: Meat

I ventured to make this recipe myself because I had tasted this, and other versions of it, several times as I was growing up. I found that one of the oldest-looking scraps of paper had this recipe written down, and it was impossible to tell from what century it was or what grandmother could have written it. I added in the onion and garlic powder because after I made it the first time, I felt it was needed. I made it twice, and the second time I coated the log twice with the egg and bread crumbs, as it is important that the coating stay on the whole time. Also, it is important to mix very well, as you don't want this log splitting up at any time. One time when my grandmother made it, she added a little tomato sauce to the pan with the water and the wine and everyone loved it, but I prefer the original version. Enjoy!

½ cup chopped onion
4 cloves garlic, peeled and smashed
¼ cup chopped green pepper
Olive oil
1 (8-ounce) can tomato sauce
2 pounds ground beef
1 pound turkey pastrami or corned beef
1 tablespoon onion powder
1 tablespoon garlic powder

Juice of 1 small lemon
Pinch of salt
½ teaspoon pepper
½ teaspoon nutmeg
½ teaspoon yellow mustard (from jar)
Unseasoned bread crumbs
2 medium eggs, beaten
¼ cup cooking wine or sherry (or water)

Sauté the onions, garlic, and green pepper over medium heat in the olive oil until the onions are transparent but not browned. Add the tomato sauce and sauté together a couple of minutes. Set saucepan aside. Combine the ground beef, onion powder, garlic powder, lemon juice, and salt, with the pepper, nutmeg, and mustard, and mix well.

Split this mixture into two logs. Flatten each log. Place the slices of pastrami or corned beef in the center and seal the logs, making sure you cover the slices inside completely. Make sure the mixture is well blended because the secret is in not having it split open during the process.

Coat each log in a beaten egg and then coat liberally in bread crumbs. Repeat the process until the log is very well coated. Brown in olive oil on all sides until almost cooked. Finally, put them in the saucepan with tomato sauce that was set aside, add a bit of water or wine, cover, and cook for 20 to 25 minutes over medium heat. It is an incredible dish, and when sliced, reveals the secret ingredients inside.

Boliche Mechado

Description: A beef roast stuffed with a variety of meats
Level: Difficult
Kosher: Meat
Passover: Yes

This particular recipe comes direct from Cuba. I really don't know if it has an origin in Spain, but it does have a strong origin from the kitchens of my family home in Havana. I still recall the scent of the cooking boliches and even remember them on our dinner table! The recipe came out divine, and the night I made it for the grandmothers' Shabbat dinner, the whole house had the aroma of my childhood! It was tricky working with the available kosher meats and substituting those in this recipe. I used a 4-pound French tender roast, and I asked the butcher to make a slit all the way through in the middle to be able to stuff it.

The first time I made it I used a spicy lamb sausage known as merguez, but I found the taste too overpowering for the roast, so the next time I used a sweet veal sausage, which worked perfectly. I also bought beef fry, which needs to be prefried a little, as well as turkey and regular pastrami. And I used ½ cup lemon juice instead of the sour oranges, which I had forgotten to buy!

I find that it is important to stay true to the original flavors, and in this recipe, it would be the cumin, bay leaf, and sour oranges – those spices are what give any recipe a classic Cuban twist.

1 (3–4-pound) French roast, slit
  through the middle
1 head of garlic, cloves peeled and
  smashed
1 teaspoon pepper
1 teaspoon oregano
1 bay leaf
Juice of 6 sour oranges (I used ½
  cup lemon juice)
½ teaspoon salt
1 teaspoon cumin

Thick sausages, deli cuts, beef fry, or
  other specialty cured meats for
  stuffing
1 cup red cooking wine
1 cup water
½ cup tomato sauce
1 carrot, sliced
8 small russet potatoes, peeled
2 eggs, hard-boiled and peeled
  (optional)

Pierce the roast all over. Mix together the garlic, pepper, oregano, bay leaf, juice, salt, and cumin, and marinate the roast overnight in the fridge in this mixture. Pour off the marinade and set aside.

Preheat oven to 350°F. Stuff the roast with the sausages and deli meats through the special slit cut through the middle. Place in a Dutch oven with some oil and brown on all sides. Add all the marinade mixture as well as the wine, 1 cup of water, and the tomato sauce. Add carrot and potatoes and cover. Bake for 3½ hours. Some cooks will add hard-boiled eggs inside the roast as well.

Cocido Madrileño

Description: A meaty stew with many layers of flavor
Level: Difficult
Kosher: Meat
Passover: Yes

This thick and hearty stew is a staple in Spain, and while some of the ingredients have been modified since the grandmothers made it in the 1700s and 1800s, it still tastes and smells exactly as I recall from my childhood. My grandmother used to ladle it up in her beautiful bowls of white china with tiny blue flowers. Almost all sources agree that this is the traditional start of the Sabbath stew from pre-Inquisition times. In Spain, this stew for the Sephardic Jews was called *adafina,* while the Ashkenazic version was known as cholent. This slow-cooking stew that started cooking on Friday afternoons was rich in varied meats, beans, and vegetables. The cocido fed the whole family on the Sabbath, when cooking was not allowed. Traditionally it contained eggs that would simmer in the stew for a long time, and the shells would turn brown. The eggs would be peeled before serving. I handed this recipe over to my really good friend Marsha Margulies. She is usually the expert baker of cakes and pies in our group so I thought I would challenge her with this huge meaty project. She came through as usual, undaunted, and modified it as per Marsha.

The recipe below shows how the original was modified with some of her changes incorporated. She made this the night we had our grandmothers' Shabbat dinner and everyone loved the stew. It was thick and very tasty. Marsha commented that she chose to make this in a huge Crock-Pot and had to cut down on the amount of ingredients because they wouldn't fit in otherwise. It can be made in a large stew pot on the stove but can also be made in the oven and cooked slowly for many hours. We have simplified it in some ways, such as using canned garbanzo beans versus dried ones, but if you have the time, it is always best to make it according to the original and authentic grandmother version.

1½ gallons water

1 pound skirt steak (Marsha used stew beef)

1 or 2 meat bones (these were left out due to space)

½ chicken, cut into 4 (Marsha used 3 large thighs)

4–5 veal or beef sausages (not the spicy ones)

1 pound smoked turkey thigh (sold in packages for shawarma)

1 (8-ounce) can garbanzo beans

8 medium eggs in their shell (Marsha used 4 eggs)

1 pound potatoes, quartered

3 onions, chopped

5 cloves garlic, peeled and left whole

½ green pepper, chopped

½ cup chopped Swiss chard

3 medium-sized carrots, cut into ½-inch rounds

6 small tomatoes, halved (Marsha also added a 28-ounce can whole tomatoes)

Salt and pepper

Put the full amount of water to boil in a large stew pot on stove. Boil all the meats together for 15 to 20 minutes. Remove the foam that forms on top of the pot. Add the garbanzo beans and bring to a boil. Add the rest of the ingredients and bring to a rolling boil. Simmer on low heat until all flavors blend. Season with salt and pepper to taste.

Hornazo

Description: A large artisanal pastry filled with varied meats
Level: Difficult
Kosher: Meat

I found it very interesting that this hornazo recipe was in all the different cookbooks of the grandmothers and also in many of the snippets of paper that were handwritten separately. All the recipes had different measurements that I had to take and combine, as some just had a word or two. This is basically a meat pie, and the recipes say it was always eaten in the fields after an important and long fast day. It was also taken on vacation as something that could be eaten every day. It originates in Ciudad Rodrigo in Spain, near Salamanca and the Duero River. It is also cooked in the same region up and down the Douro River (as the Portuguese call it) but on the Portuguese side. On this one, I naturally had to make sure all the ingredients were kosher. It is a specialty recipe that is best saved for special occasions but should be tried at least once. It's time consuming, but well worth it in the end. One of my grandmothers wrote that it must always contain eggs. The other one wrote it must never contain eggs! But all agreed that one should use the best sausage that money can buy! This has been my favorite recipe in the whole group. I made this the night I had a Shabbat dedicated to the grandmothers, and it was a big hit. The hornazo was cut into squares, and people picked it up with their hands as if eating a burger. It cooks up to be a large and hearty artisanal meat pie. It was well loved and highly recommended.

Dough
1 packet active yeast
2 tablespoons sugar
3 tablespoons warm water
3½ cups all-purpose flour

4 tablespoons olive oil
8 tablespoons dry white wine
2 tablespoons margarine
¾ cup water

Put the yeast, sugar, and warm water in a small bowl and stir until the mixture is dissolved. Add 2 tablespoons of the flour and stir. Set aside for 5 minutes.

By hand, mix the yeast mixture, the rest of the flour, olive oil, wine, margarine, and ¾ cup water. Mix until smooth. If mixture is sticky, add more flour, little by little. Cover and refrigerate for 30 minutes.

Cut the dough in half. Work with one half only as the base of the pie and reserve the other for the top. Roll out the dough to make long rectangular pieces the shape of a cookie sheet. Lay the dough down on a cookie sheet that has been covered in parchment paper and begin to build the meat pie.

Filling

5 hard-boiled eggs, sliced into eighths
½ pound meats: pastrami, corned beef, beef fry, or lamb bacon
3 small pepper steaks or thin veal slices
½ pound sausages, sliced lengthwise
½ pound chicken filling made with shredded chicken and the recipe of sofrito de pollo (optional: you can skip this step, but it gives a great taste to the other meats inside the empanada and helps moisten it)
1 large egg, lightly beaten, for egg wash (optional)

Place the sliced eggs, meats, steaks, sausages, and chicken filling on top of the dough and cover with the other piece of dough. Press the edges to seal. Make an egg wash for the top if desired. Liberally poke holes in the pie so it doesn't grow. Bake at 350° degrees for approximately 30 minutes until golden brown. Cut into squares and serve.

Picadillo

Description: A Spanish staple made with savory ground beef
Level: Medium
Kosher: Meat
Passover: Yes with modifications

What Cuban home would be complete without a good picadillo recipe? It is a staple in my home still today and the homes of all my grandmothers before me. Here it is made in the way of old Spain, with a lot of garlic and olives. The modification to add raisins came later in Cuba. In its simplest form, it is served over white rice with sweet plantains on the side. It can also be eaten alone or over potatoes, and it is used as a filling for empanadas as well. It is a rich, savory dish that, when cooked in a sofrito, features all the flavors of Spain in one dish. Exclude the cornflake or bread crumbs when preparing this for Passover.

Sofrito

1 onion, cut into small pieces
3 cloves garlic, cut small

1 green pepper, cut small
½ cup olive oil

Sauté the onion, garlic, and green pepper in the olive oil until the onion is transparent.

Picadillo

2 pounds ground beef
2 tablespoons onion powder
2 teaspoons black pepper
1 tablespoon crushed garlic
½ cup cornflake or bread crumbs
1 medium egg
1 teaspoon hot sauce

1 teaspoon cumin (I always leave
  this out; it is a typical seasoning
  in Cuban cuisine but I am not a
  fan of it)
6 large olives, crushed and cut into
  quarters
4 tablespoons dark raisins

Mix all ingredients together by hand except the olives and the raisins. Put into the saucepan with the sofrito mixture and cook until the meat is browned, stirring all the time to make sure there are no clumps in the meat. Add the olives and raisins and simmer for 20 minutes.

This is usually eaten with white rice, black beans, and fried or sweet plantains.

Ropa Vieja

Description: A shredded beef dish in a tomato base
Level: Difficult
Kosher: Meat
Passover: Yes, by leaving out the bread and cracker meal

Ropa Vieja literally means old clothes. It is a dish of a cut of beef that would break down with the long hours of cooking and resemble the shredded clothes of the poor. My family made this recipe for centuries in Spain, and it was passed down by all the grandmothers. I learned to make it at a young age, and every single woman in the family has made it at one time or another. The legend goes that this dish is over five hundred years old and a staple of the Sephardim who lived in Spain. Today, it is known as the national dish of Cuba. Funnily enough, even though it has its origins in Spain, it never caught on as a major dish there.

1 pound flank steak
2 cups full-bodied beef broth
3 tablespoons extra-virgin olive oil
1 medium yellow onion, cut small
1 green pepper, cut small
3 cloves garlic, diced
2 cups tomato sauce
Salt

3 large red pimentos, chopped small
1 tablespoon vinegar
¼ teaspoon paprika or Bijol spice mix (can be found in large supermarkets or online)
1 tablespoon cracker meal
2 to 3 slices bread
Extra olive oil for frying bread

Cook the steak in broth until tender, approximately 45 minutes. Remove steak from broth and separate into threads with your hands (versus cutting with a knife).

Heat the oil in a frying pan, then add the onion, green pepper, and garlic. When this is lightly browned, add the tomato sauce and simmer together for 10 minutes. Add the meat, salt to taste, pimentos, paprika or Bijol, and vinegar. Cook on medium heat for 15 minutes. Meanwhile, fry the bread lightly in oil. Thicken the sauce with cracker meal and serve over the fried bread.

Cuban Steak Fillets

Description: Thin steaks made the typical Cuban way
Level: Easy
Kosher: Meat
Passover: Modifiable

These were always a staple in our home in Miami, especially when we arrived from Cuba. It was a simple and economic way to make dinner in a flash by just adding white rice and maybe black beans or plantain chips. In a typical Cuban family there would always be skinny fries or fried plantains that would accompany this, but my mom was always a health fanatic even in the early '60s and would never want anything fried on the table. Because kosher meat has different cuts, I added here the suggestion to marinate so the meat would not be as tough. Just thinking about this dish evokes memories. When I found the recipe, at the bottom it says Havana, April 12, 1955.

¼ cup lemon juice
2 teaspoons yellow (prepared) mustard
½ cup finely chopped parsley

6–8 thinly sliced steaks or minute steaks
Olive oil
¼ cup finely chopped onions

Mix together the lemon juice, mustard, and parsley, reserving some parsley for the finished steaks. Marinate steaks for 6 or more hours in the lemon mixture, making sure they are fully coated.

Fry the steaks in an oiled frying pan for a couple of minutes till brown, then flip and fry the other side. Garnish with parsley and onions.

Fish

Bacalao a La Vizcaina

Description: Codfish made in the traditional way from the Vizcaya region
Level: Easy
Kosher: Pareve

The region where my family lived for 523 years is the one known in Spain as La Raya. The village of Fermoselle sits right on the Duero River, which separates Spain from Portugal. The Crypto-Jews lived up and down this Raya, which literally means line, and, in the north, where the village is, the customs, dialects, and cuisine are very similar. Codfish, which is known as bacalao in both Spanish and Portuguese, is a staple in this area. It is sold in large salted slabs at outdoor fairs and markets as well as commercial grocery stores.

I grew up eating a lot of cod, as it was a staple in my grandmother's home. She would make bacalao croquettes, bacalao soup, and tiny, compressed bacalao and potato cakes that she would fry in hot oil. What I remember the most when she made this recipe was buying the salted cod in small wooden boxes. On a recent trip to the village of my ancestors in Spain, I was surprised to see long wooden tables in the middle of the plaza selling only salted cod! This recipe sometimes includes hard-boiled eggs and raisins, but my grandmothers did not pass it down that way. It is known to be from the Basque region of Spain when cooked with potatoes. In Portugal, it is usually cooked without potatoes. The variations and nuances are minute, but someone from the region will know immediately where the recipe came from.

1 pound salted cod
2 pounds large russet potatoes, sliced
2 large onions, sliced
2 large green peppers, sliced
10 cloves garlic, crushed
¼ cup pitted green olives
2 teaspoons vinegar
⅔ cup water
1 cup dry sherry wine

⅔ cup olive oil
1 (16-ounce can) tomato sauce
½ cup small-chopped sweet red pimentos
1 loaf crusty French bread, sliced
Extra ½ cup olive oil for browning
¼ cup pitted green olives
2 teaspoons vinegar

The night before, cut the codfish into 10–12 pieces. Place in a bowl with water and cover. Change the water after 2 hours and then let sit covered in fridge for 12 hours. Next day, change the water again and simmer until the fish is tender. Let cool. Drain and separate the fish into medium-sized pieces. This is an important step to enable most of the salt to be removed.

Place the sliced potatoes in a sauté pan, and then cover with the pieces of fish. Add the onions, green peppers, garlic, olives, vinegar, water, wine, olive oil, tomato sauce, and pimentos. Cook on medium heat until the potatoes are done. Sauté the French bread in the olive oil until browned. Put bread slices on top of fish and serve over white rice.

Fish Chowder

Description: A chunky chowder made with fish and potatoes
Level: Difficult
Kosher: Pareve
Passover: Depends on your tradition

This recipe is from the Zamora region of Spain. It was given to my grandmother in the 1920s from my great-aunt Angelita. I asked my girlfriend Donna Slotsky to tackle this soup, as she is a great cook, and I knew that not everyone would want to make a fish soup. She graciously made this soup for us and brought it over for a Shabbat dinner. The soup was really tasty and liked by all. For a small group, I would cut down on the ingredients because it truly was a huge vat that she came over with that night! She stayed true to the recipe but had struggled a bit with the original version because I had translated the cut-up potato cubes as French fries. Once we cleared that up, she did a great job. Thank you, Donna! I would make this again but I would probably use milk instead of water and make it a dairy soup, adding some corn kernels and a tablespoon or so of parmesan cheese into the mix, as well as on top of the eggs. I have not attempted the dairy twist but will try for sure in the future.

1 whole, cleaned firm-flesh fish,
　　without skin and bones
1 ripe tomato, cut into quarters
1 large carrot, cut into rounds
5 cloves garlic, peeled and mashed
2 whole red onions
¼ cup parsley

1 bay leaf
10–15 freshly fried potato cubes
2 tablespoons cornstarch or potato
　　starch or tapioca
2 large hard-boiled eggs, chopped
　　small.

In a large pan, put the whole fish to boil with the tomato, carrot, garlic, onions, parsley, and bay leaf. After 20 minutes, drain in a colander. Keep only the actual flesh, cut into squares, and put back into the boiling water. Ten minutes before serving, add the starch and stir well to thicken. Fry the potato cubes in a couple of drizzles of olive oil in a saucepan. Once they are done, blend into the soup. Serve garnished with the chopped egg on top.

Snapper in Beer Sauce

Description: Snapper fish in a beer-broth base
Level: Medium
Kosher: Dairy

Once the grandmothers left Spain and moved to Cuba, the flavors of the new world started to seep into the cookbooks and recipe cards, and I could see how slowly a fish like snapper and other Caribbean fish started to take the place of cod. Beer and rum were used instead of wine, and many other subtle changes took place through the decades. Here is a typical recipe that may have initially used cod but morphed to beer and snapper in Cuba.

3 large snapper fillets
1 tablespoon water
1 teaspoon salt
⅛ teaspoon white pepper
4 tablespoons butter
½ teaspoon mustard powder
Extra ¾ teaspoon salt

¼ teaspoon Tabasco sauce
4 tablespoons flour
1 cup whole milk
½ bottle light-color beer
4 ounces gruyere-type cheese, grated
2 ounces white or farmer-type
    cheese, crumbled

Heat oven to 450°F. Cut the fillets in half and roll them up. Put them in a greased casserole. Lightly wet them with the tablespoon of water, and dust with the salt and pepper. Bake in the oven, uncovered, for 15 minutes. While they bake, melt the butter at a low heat while adding the mustard, extra salt, Tabasco sauce, and flour. Stir until a paste is formed. Gradually add the milk, stirring constantly, and then add the beer. Continue stirring until the mixture thickens. Take off the heat and add the cheeses. Mix until melted and well blended. Pour the sauce over the fillets and bake another 15 minutes or so until the sauce bubbles. Take out of oven, let the vapor subside, and serve hot and bubbly.

Side Dishes

Anise Bread

Description: Small biscuit-type breads to eat with a spread
Level: Easy
Kosher: Pareve

I always have to chuckle when I see the amount of anise liqueur that the grandmothers were putting into the recipes, and this one was no exception. The recipe for anise bread also comes from Fermoselle, and I am told it is one of the oldest recipes in the village. I asked my cousin Maji Pace Ramos to give this one a shot, and she was more than glad to do it. We share our maternal grandmother, Maneni, and this whole journey that I hit them with (we are really Jewish and not Catholic) was met with great surprise and with open arms. Not all families are as special as mine, so I am grateful that Maji also understands the importance of the revival of family memory and history. She went right out and bought her very own bottle of anise liqueur to be able to "fit right in" to the family history. She made a video of her finished product as well as her enjoying it, and as usual with all these recipes, she felt it was too eggy and needed more anise liqueur! I made them myself again with her changes, and they are below. We did have to modify the original quite a bit. So, thank you, thank you, Maji. I know how super busy she is, and it was nice to have her involved in this family project. The result is an artisanal bread to be eaten with a spread or with margarine or butter. It is a dense bread full of flavors that blend together well.

2 medium eggs

½ cup sugar

2 egg yolks

1½ cups all-purpose flour

1 teaspoon baking powder

½ cup anise liqueur

Beat the whole eggs with the sugar and slowly add the egg yolks. Mix well. Add the flour, baking powder, and liqueur until well blended.

Bake in a greased 8-inch-square pan at 350°F until golden brown. I baked approximately 45 minutes. Cut lengthwise and serve with your favorite spread.

Beet and Avocado Salad

Description: A unique salad with an interesting flavor blend
Level: Easy
Kosher: Pareve
Passover: Yes

Interestingly enough, I found this recipe repeated many times on different little pieces of paper throughout the grandmothers' books and bound journals, meaning they wanted to be sure it was not forgotten. Given the fact that it contains avocado, I figure the recipe must have been passed down after 1900, when the family moved to the Caribbean Islands and Cuba. When the grandmothers wrote this down in Spain, it was just a plain beet salad, yet the ones who were writing this in Cuba had added avocados.

In any event, I asked my friend Su Fink to take this one on in her kitchen since she is one of my few vegetarian friends, and I had found, by and large, that these recipes had practically no fruits or vegetables. Su did a great job with this one—she did not have to modify it at all, and the dressing was wonderful. The recipe was a hit with everyone!

I have a confession to make here with this recipe. I had never eaten beets in my life, and when I tasted the dish that Su made, I loved it! I have made this recipe myself many times since. The dressing is the best. I prefer using the fresh beets versus canned or packaged ones. We always try to use fresh fruits and vegetables and skip the processed foods. For Sukkot I used golden beets as well as red ones and sliced them all side by side, and it was beautiful and festive!

3 medium-sized beets
2 teaspoons salt
3 teaspoons sugar
1 large Florida avocado or three
small Hass avocados, cubed

⅓ cup olive oil
¼ cup vinegar

Wash the beets well, making sure you don't break the tail. Put in a pan, cover with water, and bring to a rolling boil. Add 1 teaspoon salt and 2 teaspoons sugar. Cover but keep on a high heat and boil for 40 minutes until soft. Take off the stove, drain, and let cool. Peel easily with your hands under running water and cut into thin slices. Place all around a large plate and put the avocado cubes in the center. Mix the oil, vinegar, and 1 teaspoon each salt and sugar. Mix well and pour over the salad as dressing. This recipe made its modern debut at the grandmothers' Shabbat and was eaten heartily by everyone there! I have made it many times since that night, as it is always enjoyed by all.

Carrot-Shaped Potatoes

Description: A fun variation on potato croquettes
Level: Easy
Kosher: Pareve

My grandmother always used to make these, and I always chuckled at the name. Basically, this is a potato recipe that is shaped like a small carrot, and in reality, could have been called potato cigars or anything else. It is a great side dish and one that I recall very well making in her kitchen. I gave this recipe over to my childhood friend Eve Murphy. Evie and I met in the third grade when we both were in Catholic school together. We continued on to high school and are still friends more years than I wish to count! I learned that Eve is an accomplished cook these days, and although I gave her a simple recipe, she made it with grace and elegance! She made her own bread crumbs (of course) from a one-day-old hard roll and added water to the mix with the eggs. She also added a sprig of parsley at the top to really look like a carrot. Eve served them with salmon, and her family told her they were strangely comforting, like matzah balls. Thank you, Eve, for cooking and using your family as taste testers.

2 pounds potatoes
1 tablespoon salt
⅛ teaspoon pepper
2 eggs, lightly beaten
Water for moistening the egg mixture

1½ cups powdered cracker crumbs or
    bread crumbs (unsalted)
Oil for frying
Parsley

Peel the potatoes and cut into cubes. Place in boiling water with the salt and cook until soft. Drain and season with the pepper and mash together. Lay out on a cold cookie sheet or on marble to cool. When the potatoes are almost cool, form a ball in your hand and make a triangular shape to look like a carrot. Coat with the beaten egg to which you have added a bit of water and then roll in the bread crumbs. Lightly fry until golden brown and attach a parsley sprig to resemble a carrot.

Beets with Oranges

Description: A tropical twist to beets
Level: Easy
Kosher: Pareve
Passover: Depends on your tradition

My colleague Carl Montoya chose to tackle this recipe, and while it seems simple enough, the ingredients should be measured carefully to make sure it is successful. Carl gave me several suggestions which I have incorporated into the recipe and instructions. Carl has always been interested in all things of Crypto-Jewish heritage and readily offered to help. I thank him for taking the time to not only make the recipe but to suggest the changes.

Beets

4 medium-sized beets
1 tablespoon cornstarch
1 cup orange juice
½ cup sugar

Orange zest
2 small oranges, peeled and sliced
Pistachio nuts, chopped (optional)

Scrub the beets, leaving the tail on to avoid bleeding. Cover beets with water, add cornstarch, juice, sugar, and zest, and boil all together until the beets are soft.

Let cool. Slice and decorate with the orange slices. Pour the dressing below over the beets and oranges. If desired, sprinkle with a few chopped pistachio nuts.

Dressing

¼ cup orange juice
2 tablespoons white vinegar

½ cup olive oil
1 tablespoon sugar

Mix all the ingredients together until well blended and pour over the beets.

Decorated Rice

Description: A tasty rice pilaf dish
Level: Easy
Kosher: Meat
Passover: Depends on your tradition

My mom used to make this often and she called it decorated rice. I always thought it was an odd name but she told me that her grandmother always called it that. When I got older, she used to call it rice pilaf. What is interesting about this recipe is that some years ago, I visited a Sephardic friend of mine in Argentina who told me this was the typical Sephardic recipe for rice handed down by the grandmothers in her family! It is a great side dish and is actually so good that it can be eaten alone.

½ cup raisins
¼ cup sweet wine
3½ cups chicken broth
2 cups long-grain rice
2½ teaspoons salt

Pinch of saffron
3 tablespoons margarine
½ cup slivered almonds, toasted in a
    frying pan
1 teaspoon cinnamon (optional)

Place the raisins in the sweet wine and set aside. Bring the chicken broth to a rolling boil. Mix in the rice, salt, saffron, and margarine. Cover and simmer until liquid is evaporated, about 20 minutes. Remove from heat, uncover, and set aside for 10 minutes or until it cools off a bit. Strain the raisins and fold the raisins and toasted almonds into the rice mixing, fluffing it up. If you wish, add the cinnamon at this time and mix in. I always leave the cinnamon out of the recipe, as I find that it is a very sharp and distinctive taste and it takes over all the other flavors of the dish.

Fruit Salad

Description: A fresh take on fruit salad
Level: Easy
Kosher: Dairy
Passover: Yes

This is a more modern recipe from Cuba, and was the one dish that was always made by my grandmother for any shower or party that she would host. I could not imagine a more traditional dish for the newer generations of the grandmothers. I have made this myself at least twenty-five times, and it is always the most refreshing dish on the buffet table. It is also the one with no leftovers! Personally, I always leave the coconut out, but my grandmother Maneni always told me it wasn't a fruit salad without the coconut! I love to share all these recipes with you because the happy memories of my childhood come flooding back. This one has the blended Caribbean fruit flavors that we grew up loving so much.

2 (8-ounce) containers rich sour cream
½ bag small kosher marshmallows
2 (8-ounce) bars cream cheese
3 small cans mandarin oranges, drained

3 cans pineapple cubes, drained
2 cans fruit cocktail, drained
1 can sliced peaches, drained
6 ounces coconut flakes

Mix the sour cream, marshmallows, and cream cheese together. Reserve the mandarin oranges from one can to decorate. Mix all the ingredients together in a glass bowl. Decorate the top of the salad with the mandarin slices. It is not wise to decorate this particular salad with cherries, as they discolor and bleed into the white salad no matter how much you dry them. You can substitute sliced real oranges for the mandarin oranges to decorate. Refrigerate and serve cool.

Pistachio Salad

Description: A sweet and pretty treat for parties or showers
Level: Easy
Kosher: Dairy
Passover: Yes

This is not a centuries-old recipe but it is one that my mom used to make all the time. There was not a card game, shower, or ladies' gathering that did not have this salad in a beautiful crystal bowl on the table. I added this here as a salute to my mom, Isabel Medina. She always was and still is an elegant, beautiful, and talented woman. She loved hosting parties of all kinds and always worked for days making and plating specialty foods. I have taken over the custom of making it, and it is not only beautiful when placed in a crystal, see-through bowl, it is also magnificent tasting!

2 (8-ounce) containers cottage cheese, large curd
1 (8-ounce) container whipped topping
1 large (20-ounce or more) can crushed pineapple

1 large or 2 small boxes pistachio pudding mix (straight from the box)
2 (12-ounce) bags walnuts

Cut the walnuts up but do not over-chop. Reserve some for decorating the top of your salad later. Mix all ingredients together and cool in refrigerator before serving. Make sure you use walnuts and not pecans, as the taste and texture will not be the same.

Garbanzo Empanadas

Description: A twist on pastry made from chick peas
Level: Easy
Kosher: Pareve or Meat

I decided to tackle this recipe myself, as I am a huge fan of garbanzo beans (chick peas) and thought it was a nice vegetarian option. I followed the recipe exactly as it was written, using a can of chick peas instead of boiling them from scratch. I formed the empanadas in my hands, and they had a very artisanal look. The recipe had called for rolling out the dough and cutting it with a cookie cutter, but I wanted that chunky look. Both ways are an option. Because it is a recipe that has very little flour, they burn quickly. I felt they were a bit dry, but my other tasters loved them. I added two tablespoons of olive oil to the mix to moisten them a bit more, but the original recipe did not call for olive oil. I served them with hummus and tahini for dipping.

1 cup fresh-cooked or canned
    garbanzo beans (chick peas)
1 cup flour
2 tablespoons margarine
1 teaspoon baking powder
½ teaspoon salt

2 tablespoons olive oil
Seasoned ground beef or ground
    chicken mixture, or a vegetarian
    option
Oil for frying (I used canola)

Grind the beans finely in a food processor with the flour, margarine, baking powder, salt, and olive oil until the dough is soft and pliable. Roll out on floured surface and cut into rounds.

I made them two ways: One I made with smaller rounds (2 inches or so). I put the meat mixture on one round and then put another round on top and pinched them together to look very artisanal. The other way, I made much larger circles (3½ inches or so). I filled them and then folded them over and made marks with the fork all around to seal.

Fry until both sides are golden brown. Yumm!

Pure de Boniato

Description: A sweet-potato side dish
Level: Easy
Kosher: Pareve
Passover: Yes

This recipe calls for the use of boniato, so I know it is from Cuba. This tuber root is used often in Cuban cuisine, and while it may be called a yam, it has a dry, white, sweet flesh. I have bought something similar also, known as a Japanese sweet potato. I love to use boniato because it is a twist on potato, and its sweet flesh changes the tone of otherwise salty stews or soupy dishes. In this recipe, I substituted margarine and pareve milk for the butter and milk. You can always revert this back to being a dairy recipe, but it will usually serve as a side dish for turkey or chicken. It is not to be missed!

2 pounds Cuban sweet potatoes, known as boniato (with white flesh): you can also use Japanese sweet potatoes as long as the flesh is white and not orange
1 cup sugar

⅛ cup margarine, melted
1 cup almond milk
2 tablespoons dry white wine
2 eggs, beaten
Raisins and almonds to taste
½ bag small kosher marshmallows

Boil and peel the boniatos. Mash together with the sugar, melted margarine, almond milk, and wine. Add the beaten eggs and blend well. Add in raisins and almonds. Fold into a greased pan and bake at 350°F for 35 minutes. Decorate with marshmallows and brown lightly in oven.

Red Sweet Peppers

Description: A marinated red pepper delicacy
Level: Easy
Kosher: Pareve
Passover: Yes

I have made this recipe many times as a side dish. It has strong flavors and is enjoyed by all. I tried making it using the red peppers that come in glass jars, but they tasted way too sharp and like preservatives. I then tried to rinse the jarred ones very well, but they still had a chemical taste. I highly recommend using fresh bell peppers. I also tried this family recipe with yellow peppers, and it did not come through as well as with red peppers. If you make it as is, you will love it!

7 large red bell peppers
1 cup white vinegar
1 cup water

1 cup sugar
Olive oil

Peel the red peppers, take out all the seeds, and cut into slices. Boil together with the rest of ingredients until all the liquid evaporates and a sweet sauce remains. Place in refrigerator with the sauce to marinate. Serve at room temperature with some olive oil drizzled over them.

Stuffed Eggplant

Description: An interesting variation on eggplant
Level: Easy
Kosher: Pareve
Passover: Yes

This is one of the few cooked vegetable recipes that were left by the grandmothers. I was lucky to at least have a few of them because nowadays I have so many vegetarian friends! When I first contacted my colleague and friend Schulamith Halevy, she readily agreed. I was thrilled because Schulamith has spent the greater part of her life helping the descendants of the Conversos of the Iberian Peninsula to return to their ancestry, and she is a world-renowned historian. She travels the world constantly, and for this project, engaged her daughter, Erga, to make this recipe. She prepared the recipe exactly as the grandmothers preserved it. She made it at home for a Shabbat meal, and everyone loved it. So here it is with no modifications. I would like to point out that there is no stuffing in this eggplant, but for authenticity's sake, staying true to the original recipes, I did not want to change the name. Enjoy! Thank you, Erga!

1 large eggplant
¼ cup olive oil
1 large white onion, chopped small
1 clove garlic, chopped small
1 cup tomato juice (or use tomato sauce, but water it down)
½ teaspoon oregano

½ teaspoon basil
Salt and pepper
2 tablespoons jarred sweet red pimentos, cut small for decorating
2 tablespoons finely chopped parsley, for decorating

Cut the unpeeled eggplant into cubes approximately 1 inch square. Heat the oil in a large saucepan on medium-high heat. Add the onion and garlic and sauté until golden. Add the cubes of eggplant and sauté together for five minutes. Add the tomato juice, oregano, and basil, and stir together. Heat to simmer and cover. Cook for 10 minutes or until the eggplant is tender but firm and still maintains its cube shapes. Add salt and pepper to taste. Decorate with the red pimentos and parsley.

Sopa de Crema

Description: A rich and creamy soup base
Level: Easy
Kosher: Dairy

This is one of the most delicious and easiest recipes that the grandmothers passed down. This simple cream soup base is wonderful to make for any type of vegetable soup. I have used it to make asparagus and broccoli soups, and the results were absolutely divine. I tried making a pumpkin soup, but it was way too heavy a base for such a dense vegetable. I am looking forward to trying cauliflower and other vegetables. The grandmothers made a point of adding that the pepper should always be white so as not to add unnecessary speckles to the soup! I hope you enjoy this as much as my family has.

4 tablespoons butter
4 tablespoons flour
1½ teaspoons salt
⅛ teaspoon white pepper

4 cups whole milk
1 teaspoon onion juice
1 to 2 cups vegetable of your choice, cooked and finely chopped

Melt the butter in a saucepan over medium heat, slowly adding the flour, salt, and pepper. Mix together until well blended. Add the milk gradually until the mixture is soft and creamy. Add the onion juice and the chopped vegetables. If you want to have a creamier soup, pass your vegetable through a food processer and blend into the soup.

Sweet Carrots

Description: A perfect side dish for Sukkot
Level: Easy
Kosher: Pareve
Passover: Yes

Through the years, I have made this recipe many times, sometimes using honey and other times as shown, with sugar. I usually will make it for Sukkot, and it is a great side dish loved by all. It is a tradition to eat sweet foods and vegetables for this holiday, and this dish is perfect. I prefer to use fresh carrots for this recipe, as the look is so much more realistic and fun.

12 small carrots, peeled, or two cans
    of small carrots
1 teaspoon salt (if using canned,
    better not to add salt)
6 tablespoons sugar

¼ pound margarine
1 tablespoon finely chopped parsley
¼ cup vegetable broth
¼ cup white wine

If using fresh carrots, boil with the salt until they are soft. Take off the stove and strain well. If using canned carrots, be sure you wash and drain them well to remove the added liquids. Melt the margarine in a sauté pan and add the sugar until well mixed. Leave on low until the mixture takes on a light caramel color. Add the parsley and carrots. Sauté gently and then add the broth and white wine. Cook on high heat for 2 to 3 minutes and serve warm.

Torrejas

Description: A variation on French toast
Level: Easy
Kosher: Dairy

My dad always worked very hard and was out of the house every single day at the crack of dawn, but the fondest memories I have of him are the big breakfasts that he always made for us on Sundays. He used to wake up early and put together a feast like no other, and many times he used to make this grandmothers' recipe for us. The only difference was that my dad never used the liqueur. I miss my dad but his warmth and sweetness live on in recipes like this one.

1 cup whole milk
6 large slices thick bread, with
    no crust, but preferably not
    sourdough because of its strong
    flavor

3 to 4 medium eggs
Oil for frying
Almibar (see recipe below)

Place the milk in a shallow pan and quickly submerge the bread slices one by one in the milk. Gently squeeze out the liquid from each piece and place on a flat tray. Beat the eggs together with a fork until frothy. Dip the slices one by one in the egg and drain slightly. Heat the oil and fry the slices until-golden brown on both sides. Drain on paper towels. Place in a serving dish and pour the almibar on top. Leave to cool at room temperature.

Almibar

Almibar is a basic sugar syrup that is used as a base and a liquid topping for most Spanish desserts. While it is usually made with white sugar and water, sometimes honey, thinned with water, is used as well.

1 cup water
2 cups sugar

¼ cup sambuca or anise liqueur (not anise essence)

Place the water and sugar in a small saucepan on medium heat until it comes to a rolling boil, and then lower the temperature for 3 minutes. Take off the heat and mix in the liqueur. Cool slightly and pour over the torrejas.

Tortilla Española

Description: The typical thick Spanish omelet
Level: Easy
Kosher: Pareve
Passover: Yes

If you ask anyone to mention just one food that Spain is known for, I imagine it would be tortilla. This is the iconic food of Spain – and the only dish made and sold everywhere there. I chose my friend and colleague Debbie Wohl-Isard to make this because she is very involved with the whole Crypto-Jewish movement and is in fact the editor of *La Granada,* the online newsletter of the Society for Crypto-Judaic Studies. Debbie did not vary the ingredients and told me it reminded her of a frittata! I am certain she did justice to this important Spanish recipe!

4 large potatoes (use russet or golden ones)
½ cup olive oil
Salt and pepper

1 large white onion (optional), cut into rings
10 to 12 medium eggs

Peel and cut potatoes into ¼-inch slices. Cook in hot oil for 15 to 20 minutes until tender. When done, move them to a bowl and dust with salt and pepper to taste. Reserve 4 tablespoons from the leftover oil and cook the onion until soft and golden brown.

Whisk the eggs well in a large bowl, then add the potatoes and onions. Mix gently.

Pour the egg mixture into the oil in the pan and cook over medium heat for 8 to 10 minutes or until it has started to set and the bottom is golden brown. Gently put a spatula under the tortilla until you feel most of it lift off, and then put a large plate over it and turn it upside-down. (Many times I have put the pan under the oven broiler to cook the top rather than risk it breaking.) Slide into the pan for another 4 or 5 minutes.

Serve at room temperature in pie-shaped wedges.

Vegetable Soufflé

Description: A healthy blend of vegetables
Level: Easy
Kosher: Dairy or Pareve

My friend Bini Masin cooks the healthiest food, and while I started her off on a different recipe, she politely came back to me for one with no oil, sugar, or flour, which was hard given that most of the grandmothers' recipes were chock-full of all the above. I did find this dairy recipe with some vegetables, and Bini made it for Shabbat. She decided to make it pareve, so I have listed her changes below. Bini did say that she thinks it would have been better to keep the original dairy version, as it would have made a richer finished product. Thank you, Bini, for always keeping us a little bit healthier!

4 medium eggs, separated
1½ cups boiling-hot milk (Bini used almond milk)
1 cup diced bread
1 onion, chopped finely
½ cup grated cheese (Bini used soy cheese)
2 tablespoons chopped parsley
3 tablespoons chopped red pimentos

⅛ pound butter, melted (Bini used margarine)
1½ teaspoons salt
¼ teaspoon pepper
½ cup chopped Swiss chard
1 cup sweet peas
½ cup pumpkin puree
½ cup small-chopped asparagus, fresh or bottled

Mix the egg whites until foamy like snow and set aside. In a large mixing bowl, place the hot milk, bread, onion, cheese, parsley, pimentos, butter, salt, and pepper. Add the egg yolks one by one and mix well. Add the egg whites and mix well. Add all the other vegetables and mix gently until combined. Fold into a greased Pyrex baking pan and bake at 350°F for 1 hour. Serve hot.

Sauces

Almond Sofrito from Fermoselle

Description: A sautéed base for many dishes from Fermoselle, made with almonds
Level: Easy
Kosher: Pareve

This almond sauce was passed down to my mother from her mother and is the recipe of my great-grandmother Maria Flores Alvarez. It was passed down to her by her mother, Maria Alvarez Garrido, and her mother before her, Teresa Garrido Mayor. She started practically each and every dish with this sauce, and it was taken on by my grandmother as her own, and so on down the family. I chose to give this recipe to my colleagues Jesus Jambrina and Alfredo Estenoz. Jesus has been investigating the past Jewish heritage of the Zamora region, where my family lived for centuries, and we met when I attended his first academic conference. Jesus has won many important accolades for his work and is an academic and published author. He and Alfredo direct Centro Isaac Campanton, which they established to recuperate the Jewish legacy in the region of Zamora where my family is from, and both work tirelessly to preserve our Jewish memories.

Jesus made the recipe below and told me that it was incredibly delicious! He used much less saffron (a pinch only). After making the sofrito, he sautéed chicken chunks in it, and it was divine! He will use this often now as a base in his cooking. This is a twist on the typical sofrito recipe that you will see often in this book. Thank you so much, Jesus and Alfredo, for making one of my favorite recipes come to life again. I am certain that your homes were as fragrant with these Spanish scents as my grandmothers' homes were for centuries.

12 cloves garlic, peeled
22 shelled almonds, whole and
     unroasted
7 teaspoons chopped toasted fresh
     oregano (to bring out flavor)

1 tablespoon saffron
2 slices bread, toasted and crumbled
1 small tomato (optional)
Olive oil

Chop all ingredients finely and sauté in the olive oil until the ingredients are well blended for a thick, aromatic mixture that can be used as a base for any meat or chicken dish. My grandmothers never used the tomato in their own recipe but always added that it was optional!

Almibar

Description: A thick sugar sauce with many flavor variations
Level: Easy
Kosher: Pareve
Passover: Yes (if using kosher for Passover flavorings)

Almibar is the sugar sauce that is used over many desserts in Spain. Depending on the region, the almibar recipe will vary, appearing in many different flavors.

2 cups water
1 cup sugar

1 tablespoon rum, or another liqueur
(my family always used anise)
1 tablespoon orange or lemon zest

Mix all ingredients together over medium-high heat, stirring constantly until a heavy syrup is formed. Take great care not to over-boil it, as it will turn gritty.

Cuban Sofrito

Description: The typical starter base for most meat and chicken dishes
Level: Easy
Kosher: Pareve
Passover: Yes

Sofrito is the basis of all Spanish cooking, including Cuban cooking. You will have noticed by now that Cuban and Spanish-Portuguese cuisine does not include anything spicy. Many people think of Spanish food as always spicy but it just isn't so. Our foods are layered with many flavors, including garlic, onions, green peppers, and many times fresh tomatoes and olive oil. Sofrito is fragrant, and I never start any dish without this. Interestingly enough, all the grandmothers, as far back as I could see, used a sofrito in their recipes but with some variations. Not only does it make all the meat dishes taste the specific way that they do, but it also makes your kitchen smell like old-world cooking. I know that when my own home is infused with a great sofrito scent, it feels like the good old days!

Olive oil
1 onion, chopped small
¼ green pepper, chopped small
5 large cloves garlic, crushed and
   sliced

½ cup tomato sauce
½ cup white cooking wine

Heat up a couple of drizzles of olive oil in a medium-hot frying pan and add the onion, green pepper, and garlic. Sauté until the onions are transparent, then add the tomato sauce and wine. Simmer on low heat for 10 minutes and set aside while preparing the meat or chicken that uses this as a base.

Fresh Tomato Sauce

Description: The freshest tomato sauce, with many savory flavors
Level: Easy
Kosher: Pareve
Passover: Yes

It's not only the Italians who like a good tomato sauce! In our home, and in the homes of the grandmothers before me, the tomato sauce was always made from scratch, and this is their (and my) specialty tomato sauce. You can make this in large batches and freeze. You will never again reach for the jar of tomato sauce at the supermarket once you have tried this special sauce.

25 ripe tomatoes, cut into quarters
1 onion, finely chopped
1 clove garlic, diced
4 sweet red pimentos

½ cup water
1 teaspoon salt, or more, to taste
2 teaspoons sugar
2 teaspoons lemon juice

Put all ingredients except sugar and lemon juice in a large saucepan and bring to a boil. Continue cooking at a rolling boil for 12 minutes. Take off the stove and strain immediately (the tomato skins will be left behind). Add the sugar and the lemon juice to the sauce. Use this sauce over chicken or spaghetti, or you can add cooked merguez or turkey sausages right into the sauce and serve over white rice.

Onion Sauce

Description: A hearty sauce to use as a base or serve over many dishes
Level: Medium
Kosher: Pareve or dairy

What is Spanish cuisine without a good onion sauce to use over a plain chicken, or a vegetable, spaghetti, or any other side dish? This is one of my favorite sauce recipes, and while I have listed it as pareve, the ingredients can quickly be switched up to be dairy. This is a rich and yummy sauce that I have made many times.

2 tablespoons margarine
½ teaspoon olive oil
2 tablespoons flour
1 cup pareve, unflavored milk
½ teaspoon salt

⅛ teaspoon pepper
½ teaspoon nutmeg
½ cup grated onion
1 tablespoon lemon juice

Melt the margarine and olive oil over a low heat and add the flour until well blended. Add the milk, slowly stirring to a simmer until the sauce is smooth and has a good consistency – not too liquid. Add the salt, pepper, and nutmeg, and mix slowly. Add the onion and simmer for 2 to 3 more minutes. Take off the stove, mix in the lemon juice, and serve hot. The recipe can be made with butter, whole milk, and grated cheese instead of onion to serve over vegetables or any other side dish.

Sweet Onions

Description: A specialty recipe for onion lovers
Level: Easy
Kosher: Pareve
Passover: Yes

This simple-to-make recipe is a great side dish for the onion lovers. I wrote it out like the grandmothers had it for one pound of small yellow onions, but truth be told, I generally will make 5 pounds or more at a time and store in the fridge for the next few meals. Soooo good!

¼ pound butter or margarine
1 pound small yellow onions

Sugar

Peel the onions and put in a large rectangular Pyrex or aluminum container. Cover with water. Cut the butter or margarine into squares and place on top of onions. Sprinkle liberally with sugar. Bake at 400°F until the onions are browned. Serve as a side dish to fish, meats, and chicken.

Desserts

Aceitadas

Description: A dense cookie, similar to shortbread
Level: Medium
Kosher: Pareve

This is a recipe from one of my great aunts, Angelita, from the Zamora region of Spain, where the family lived for centuries. She sent this recipe in the 1920s to my grandmother, who made it many times, and it has been preserved to this day. These cookies were usually eaten during Holy Week (the week leading up to Easter Sunday), and, along with many of the desserts in this book, are considered artisanal. I made these melt-in-your-mouth cookies a couple of times, and the ingredients list and instructions below already reflect the modern tweaking of the recipe. They remind me a bit of shortbread, and while they are a bit oily (*aceite* means oil), these are the *best* cookies ever! The ever-present anise is in the recipe but I think any liqueur flavor can be substituted.

4¼ cups olive oil
3 cups sugar
1 cup anise liqueur (not anise essence)
6 eggs, separated

5½ pounds flour
1 teaspoon baking powder
¼ cup sugar for brushing
Jelly (optional)

Mix the oil, sugar, liqueur, and egg yolks together until well blended. Then start slowly adding the flour and the baking powder. Mix by hand until you can make balls that are about 1½ inches wide. Mark a star shape in the center of each with your knife. Mix 3 egg whites with ¼ cup of sugar and brush tops before baking. Bake at 350°F for 20 minutes or until golden brown. You may wish to add a tiny bit of jelly in the center for color.

Almendrados

Description: An almond pastry
Level: Easy
Kosher: Pareve
Passover: Yes

Here is another almond pastry recipe. My family used almonds in many of their recipes, including as a base for meat and chicken. The region they were from had many almond trees, which you can still see growing there today. My friend Fay Weinberg offered to bake this one, and as she is not an almond lover, I have to truly thank her for going the extra mile. Below is the original recipe and in parentheses I put the amounts that Fay used to make these incredible, special delicacies. The hardest thing about the recipe, according to Fay, was finding kosher almond paste! I put the original measurements and then the ones that Fay used. I saw that hers worked well, and perhaps the original would have also, but it would have had a lot more sugar.

16 ounces almond paste — not almond butter (Fay used 12 ounces)
16 ounces confectioners' sugar (Fay used 8 ounces)

1 teaspoon cinnamon
Zest of one lemon
2 egg whites

Mix all together to form a paste that is neither too soft nor too hard. Form little bars approximately 3 inches long and bake at 350°F for 19 to 20 minutes until hardened. Little designs may be made on the top with a fork, or you can leave them plain. We ate these the night of the grandmothers' Shabbat, and they were amazing! Thanks, Fay!

Almond Horns

Description: A traditional horn-shaped almond pastry
Level: Easy
Kosher: Pareve
Passover: Yes, if you can find almond paste kosher for Passover or make your own at home

These delicious almond pastries were taught to me by my grandmother when I was very young. I recall taking the almond paste and working it through my small hands and forming tiny little balls or almond horns with it. I was so surprised after converting to Judaism and participating in my first set of High Holidays that almond horns were being made and sold in the Jewish bakeries. I still make these for the holidays and especially for Rosh Hashanah.

16 ounces almond paste
16 ounces confectioners' sugar
Sprinkling of cinnamon

Zest of one whole lemon
2 egg whites
8 ounces slivered almonds

Mix together the almond paste, sugar, cinnamon, and zest together, then add 1 of the egg whites until the mixture is semi-hard. I always mix the ingredients with my hands as I was taught. Use the 2nd egg white if needed. Shape the mixture into horns or small balls and roll in slivered almonds until fully covered. Bake on a cookie sheet at 350°F for

15 minutes. Watch them carefully, as they can burn easily, especially on the bottom. It helps to use parchment paper on the cookie sheet to prevent burning.

This Passover, I wanted to make these, and though I hunted high and low, I was not able to find almond paste that was certified kosher for Passover. During this holiday, we don't bring anything into our kitchens that is not certified specially for use during Passover because the product could have mixed with flour or other products that would not belong in our kitchens during this time.

I decided to go ahead and make them anyway, but to do that, I bought 5 pounds of raw almonds, blanched them for a few minutes in boiling water, took the peels off with my fingers, passed them through the food processor with confectioners' sugar, and made my own almond paste! They formed beautifully into the almond horns. I also made cookies with marmalade in the center. Where there is a will, there is always a way. I will say that they tasted by far better and fresher than the canned almond paste but were very labor intensive.

Anise Torticas

Description: An airy cookie with anise as the star ingredient
Level: Medium
Kosher: Dairy

Anise is one of those aromatic spices that you either love or you hate. Whichever the case is, many of the recipes from my ancestral town of Fermoselle use anise. It was used in teas to aid digestion, in meats, and mostly in dessert recipes. It grows rampant in Turkey but the Spaniards say the best of the world's anise flowering plants are found in Spain. In my grandmother's book it says that as the cookies bake in the oven, one is supposed to sing a little Spanish children's song, "Las Torticas." It gladdens my heart to see the happiness that pours out through the well-worn pages.

When my very close friend Su Fink asked me for a recipe, I gave her this one, and I can totally say that she rocked it! The cookies were amazing and perfect for dunking into a café con leche. She cautions that we should use even more anise, so the recipe was modified to give that kicky anise flavor. After all, what is an anise cookie without anise? Thank you, Su, for making this happen – especially since you aren't an anise lover! She brought the finished cookies to our special grandmothers' Shabbat dinner, and the cookies flew! She told me recently that she has made it again and again for her family.

Here is the original dairy version.

1 pound butter
1 pound sugar
3 teaspoons liquid anise extract
3 eggs, lightly beaten

1½ teaspoons baking soda
  (bicarbonate)
2 pounds all-purpose flour

Here is the pareve version that Su made while cutting the recipe in half. I only tasted this version, and the cookies were great!

1 cup oil
¾ cup sugar
2 to 3 teaspoons anise extract
2 medium eggs, lightly beaten

¾ teaspoon baking soda
  (bicarbonate)
3⅓ cups flour

Cream together the butter (or oil) with the sugar and add the anise while mixing well. Mix in the eggs and the baking soda, and then the flour, while continuing to mix well by hand. When all is well mixed, form little cookies in the palm of your hand, place on a greased cookie sheet, and bake at 350°F for 15 minutes until golden brown.

Almond Crown

Description: A Bundt cake with a heavy almond base
Level: Difficult
Kosher: Pareve

This is another recipe from Fermoselle that was always made for the holidays. I tried it out, and it was excellent. I baked it in a flower-shaped Bundt pan, and it was not only beautiful but felt very festive. When it was finished, I drizzled the honey on top, and it looked like a professional dessert. My grandmother served this dessert many times in her home, and it always looked elegant.

6 medium to large eggs, separated
¼ cup butter
¾ cup sugar
1 cup flour
1 tablespoon baking powder

Lemon zest
3.5 ounces (100 grams) crushed almonds
2 ounces dark honey for drizzling
4 ounces slivered almonds, toasted

Whip the egg whites with a little bit of sugar and set aside. Beat the butter and sugar together and slowly add the egg yolks, flour, baking powder, lemon zest, and crushed almonds. Fold in the egg whites and place in a lightly greased Bundt pan. Bake at 350°F until a knife inserted in the center comes out clean.

Unmold and drizzle the honey mixed with almonds over the top.

Azucarado Hervido

Description: A glaze or frosting for cakes
Level: Difficult
Kosher: Pareve
Passover: Yes

The literal translation of *azucarado hervido* is boiled sugar. In reality, this recipe is to be used as a coating or a frosting for cakes or even biscuits. The honey is optional. My grandmother wrote in her notes that she used to eat it by itself and she remembered when her great-grandmother used to make it. She also told me that using honey, the frosting was creamier and smooth for much longer. She actually had written this recipe out twice. The one with honey she called Glase and the one without was titled Boiled Sugar! A very basic recipe that can be used with any one of various flavors added.

2 cups granulated sugar
1 cup water
2 tablespoons honey (optional)
2 egg whites, beaten to snowy peaks

1 teaspoon any essence such as
  lemon, orange, or anise
¼ teaspoon baking powder

Boil the sugar with the water, stirring with a wooden spoon until a thread can separate from the spoon. Pour slowly over the egg whites. Add the essence and honey, and continue mixing until the mixture is thickened and becomes cold. Add the baking powder and continue mixing. This makes a sufficient quantity for coating a large cake or a three-layer cake.

Bizcochos

Description: A hard cookie to be eaten with a fruit spread
Level: Medium
Kosher: Pareve

One of the things I enjoyed the most when I visited my grandparents was the sense of total peace and relaxation that I always felt in their home. I wonder about that today and have tried to recreate it in my own home, but I've found it impossible with all the running around that we do these days. These bizcochos that my grandmother used to make were always eaten in the kitchen with a large cup of café con leche. How I long for one more day with them at their little table. I understand now that it wasn't that they weren't busy or that they were bored; rather, they put everything aside and gave me their undivided attention. I learned the art of listening through this recipe. Because of this important family history and the art of listening, I gave this recipe over to Yael Trusch, also known as the Jewish Latin Princess. I met Yael when she asked me to be on one of her podcast shows, and we have been in close touch ever since. She is a dynamo of a woman and a role model all the way. She does podcasts as well as videos and so much more. She is always empowering women to draw on their own strengths and beauty. A special lady with a big heart. Yael went the extra mile with this, and not only did she have to keep running back and forth to the store for more margarine, she also had to make it a couple of times, tweak it, and remake it. She feels it is now perfect! Like most of the other recipes of the grandmothers, this was coming out way too eggy, so she modernized it and reworked it! Below is the new and best updated version of the egg biscuits. Thank you so much, Yael. You are a true Jewish Latin Princess in more ways than one!

2 ½ cups all-purpose flour
1 teaspoon baking powder
1 cup (2 sticks) margarine (or butter
    if you want it dairy), at room
    temperature
2 egg yolks

1 teaspoon vanilla extract
1 cup sugar (¾ for dough and ¼ for
    sprinkling)
½ teaspoon orange extract or other
    flavoring
Preheat oven to 325°F.

Mix together the flour and baking powder, and slowly add the margarine. Mix well. Slowly incorporate the egg yolks and vanilla, and finally the ¾ cup sugar and orange extract. The mixture should be soft. Roll out on a lightly floured surface and cut the cookies into circles or shapes with a cookie cutter. I still prefer to cut them with the rim of a glass as my grandmother used to. However, Yael rolled the dough inside parchment paper (to prevent sticking) into long cylinders 1-to-2 inches in diameter and then sliced the cookie dough into ¼-inch slices. As you can see, I am still sentimental about the ways of the grandmothers, but I am certain that the way Yael cut them up is much more practical!

Line 2 cookie sheets with parchment paper, place the slices on them, and bake for 20 minutes or until golden brown, depending on your oven. Sprinkle with sugar and enjoy!

Bollo Maimon

Description: A light and fluffy Bundt cake
Level: Medium
Kosher: Pareve
Passover: Yes

My grandmother always told me this was a recipe from Salamanca, which is a large city a bit south of Fermoselle and an hour and a quarter drive. These are still all Spanish recipes but I find it interesting that my grandmother made the distinction that this particular one was NOT from Fermoselle. I find this to be an unusual recipe in that it can be used for Passover because there is no flour. My grandmother also told me that it could be eaten after any meal. I did not understand at the time but that means that the recipe is pareve and not dairy, as the Jewish dietary laws do not allow milk to be eaten after a meat meal. This may well have been one of the original Sephardic cakes. The name of the famous Jewish Sage, Maimonides, was Rabbi Moshe Ben Maimon. Is there a correlation? We will never know, but if there is no connection, then it is truly an odd name for a cake! I gave this recipe to Laura Garcia from Valen Productions in Miami, who has been incredible in the promotion of my Spanish books. Laura has been my number one fan from the day I wrote my first book about the fifteen grandmothers (I have since traced back to find twenty-two grandmothers!). She has been patiently waiting for this cookbook for a couple of years. I was excited to give Laura this very special recipe, and the measurements below indicate the changes and tweaks that she made. I saw pictures of this cake, and it was stunning! She told me it was so good and eaten quickly in her home. *Gracias,* Laura!

Note that this recipe originally specified "1 ounce of sugar and starch for each egg used." Because of the difficulty of following the ancient recipe, I have converted this to definite amounts.

10 medium eggs
1 cup cornstarch or potato starch
2 teaspoons baking powder

1 cup confectioners' sugar, plus extra
 for decoration

Separate the eggs and beat the whites until they form peaks. Mix all the other ingredients well, including the egg yolks. Fold in the egg whites and place in a greased Bundt pan (according to the grandmothers, it was preferable if the pan was copper, but Laura used a Teflon Bundt pan, and it worked great). Bake at 350°F for 30 to 40 minutes or until a knife inserted in the center comes out clean. Sprinkle with powdered sugar on top.

Bollos de Leche

Description: A confection similar to a sugar doughnut
Level: Easy
Kosher: Dairy

My girlfriend Sandi Samole made this a *motza'ei Shabbat* project, and she said they were delicious! She used a liquid shortening and canola oil. Because the shortening was liquid, she felt she had to add more flour, but in the end they fried up quickly, and when fried, looked and tasted a lot like donut holes. While they were still hot, she twirled them in granulated sugar. Beautiful and delicious! Sandi is a well-known interior designer and she made these with as much grace and elegance as she does the homes she decorates. Thank you, Sandi. I know you are a super busy person and I really appreciated your time.

1 cup liquid vegetable shortening
1 cup milk
1 cup flour, plus some

Canola oil for frying
¼ cup white granulated sugar

Mix the shortening with the milk and add the flour little by little until you can form a ball in your hand. Do not use more flour than you need. Drop the balls into hot oil and fry until golden brown. Twirl in the sugar.

Buñuelos del Viento

Description: Fried dough with a typical Spanish flavor
Level: Medium
Kosher: Dairy

I gave this recipe to my girlfriend Jackie Attias. I think Jackie is one of the best Sephardic cooks I know, so I was anxious to hear her comments about this recipe. She told me it reminded her of *sfinge*, which is basically a Moroccan donut that is popular around Chanukah time or the Mimouna party at night immediately at the end of Passover. Her comments follow, and the recipe has been modified to reflect her changes. "They came out delicious, as good as any yeast dough! It was a sticky dough, so I refrigerated it for half an hour and dropped odd-shaped dumplings with a spoon rather than forming into balls. They came out light and wonderful. Worth the carbs! Would do it again!"

2 cups water
2 tablespoons butter
Zest of 1 lemon
Pinch of salt

5 tablespoons sugar
2½ to 3 cups flour
3 to 6 medium to large eggs
Oil for frying

Boil all ingredients except the flour and eggs for five minutes. Slowly add the flour and mix well until the mixture separates from the pan. Let cool and slowly add up to 6 eggs until you can form small balls or drop by spoonfuls into the hot oil. Fry until golden brown and serve alone or drizzled with honey or granulated sugar.

Buñuelos de Yuca

Description: A typical Cuban fried delicacy made from yuca (cassava)
Level: Difficult
Kosher: Dairy

My great-grandmother Maria, who lived in Madrid all her life, had been born to parents who were originally from the small ancestral village of Fermoselle. She married a man who chartered ships and managed a great business shipping building materials between Spain and Cuba. He would take concrete and construction materials to Cuba at the turn of the century and return to Spain with fine, exotic woods from the small island nation. She continued to live in Madrid and often visited Cuba, where my great-grandfather had settled and bought several plantations. In 1908, when she was expecting my grandmother, she went to Cuba for a visit, and my grandmother was born there. Eventually, the family settled in the east coast of Cuba while the rest of the family stayed in Spain. The recipe below comes from that early time in Cuba and is made with yuca, a tuberous root that grows underground and is somewhat similar to a potato, yet much more fibrous and stringy.

Today, yuca is available fresh just about anywhere that has a Caribbean, Central American, or Cuban population. It is widely eaten in desserts and side dishes throughout the Caribbean and the rest of Latin America as well. With all this in mind, I handed this recipe over to my Cuban friend Lissette Valdes-Valle. Lissette comes from a background similar to mine and is very active in the Jewish community. Who better to try a Cuban recipe than my Juban friend? She is one of the most excitable people I know. Nothing wallflower about her, and it is with that great enthusiasm that she launched into this project and took pictures along the way at every step. Thank you, *mi amiga!* I am so glad you were able to enjoy it while honoring our past and traditions!

Buñuelos

2 pounds fresh yuca
2 medium eggs
½ cup milk
Pinch of salt

1 tablespoon sugar
¼ to ½ cup all-purpose flour
½ teaspoon baking powder
Oil for frying

Peel the yuca and cut into small pieces to make it easier to boil until fully cooked. Drain well and put in a mixing bowl. Add eggs, milk, salt, and sugar, and mix well with a fork while mashing the yuca. Cover the bowl and set aside to cool for 15 to 20 minutes. Mash well together and add flour and baking powder little by little, adding only enough to be able to form small balls. The recipe calls for using a range of flour amounts depending on the consistency you want. If you wish the buñuelos to taste more like yuca, then add less flour. If you want them to taste more like a donut, then add more flour.

Fry the balls in hot oil and drain. Serve with syrup (almibar) flavored with anise or another liqueur. My family always used anise but it makes every single recipe taste like the other, so I try to keep the use of anise down! Lissette tells me that she poked holes in the little balls after frying to be sure the almibar infused the buñuelos throughout. Lissette had a great time making these, and her family licked their fingers for days to come!

Almibar

2 cups water
1 cup sugar
1 tablespoon rum or another liqueur
    (my family always used anise)

1 tablespoon orange or lemon zest

Mix all ingredients together over medium-high heat, stirring constantly until a heavy syrup is formed. Take great care not to over-boil it, as it will turn gritty.

Chiricaya

Description: A pudding originating in the Canary Islands
Level: Difficult
Kosher: Dairy
Passover: Yes

This pudding-like recipe was passed down by the family of my paternal grandmother, Mati. One side of her family settled in Cartago, Costa Rica, in the late 1700s and had immigrated there from Cartagena, Colombia. Many of that branch of the family are still living in Cartago today, several hundred years later. I have only seen this recipe as traditional Costa Rican cuisine and with a history of being eaten only on Holy Week. It is interesting that many of the recipes from both the grandmothers that are typically eaten on Holy Week are also Passover recipes with no flour. Many new communities of Crypto-Jews are coming out in Costa Rica these days, and of course, I will always jump to the conclusion that these old recipes started as Passover recipes for the Crypto-Jews. Devorah Zachariah, who is originally from the Dominican Republic and my longtime friend, took this one on during Passover. Devorah has always suspected she has a strong Crypto-Jewish lineage and for the last twenty years or so has graced our Passover Seders with not only her presence but with beautifully decorated trays of salads and fruit. Her attention to detail is amazing, and this time it was no different. She placed the molded chiricaya in the center of a white glass plate, decorated all around with orange slices and kiwi slices on top of that. She grated orange and lemon peel and decorated the top of the plate like confetti. For her taste, this was too sweet, and she tells me it is very important to add the citrus zest. For me, I found it perfect. Thank you, Devorah, for bringing the bar up a notch!

2 cups milk
1 cinnamon stick
¼ teaspoon cinnamon powder
½ cup sugar

2 tablespoons sweet red wine
2 medium eggs
½ teaspoon vanilla extract
Zest of 1 lemon

In a saucepan, mix together the milk, cinnamon stick, cinnamon powder, and sugar. Bring to a boil and let it boil for exactly 4 minutes. Take off the burner and let it cool slightly. Pass the mixture through a strainer to get rid of any leftover cinnamon or milk skin. Set aside. In blender or food processor, blend well the wine, eggs, vanilla, and ½ cup of the milk mixture. When fully blended, add the rest of the milk mixture. Pour into small (3-inch), greased, ovenproof ramekins (makes 10 to 12) or into a greased, shallow Pyrex pan set into a water bath (a pan of water underneath the baking pan or ramekins). Bake at 350°F for 60 minutes or until golden brown. You may sprinkle cinnamon or lemon zest on top. The finished product has a consistency somewhere between a flan and a pudding.

Chuletas – Tia Paulita

Description: A unique Crypto-Jewish presentation for a French toast creation
Level: Medium
Kosher: Dairy

I think this recipe is the one that caused me the most angst to find and then sheer delight at the end. I will now share it with you.

This recipe was finally written down by my great-aunt Tia Paulita, who was born in the 1880s and never married. She was an elegant lady, always dressed to the nines, and was known for being the best cook of the family. She had been passing down the recipe again and again, and always made it from memory until it was finally written down by the family on the day she died, in Madrid, Spain, in 1936.

Chuleta means "pork chop" in Spanish, and even though my family was Catholic for five hundred years and they ate all types of foods, I still got a sinking feeling in my stomach every time I opened my grandmom's cookbook and saw the word *chuleta* on page 2. For months, I could not bring myself to read it. When I finally did start to read and the first line said to add milk to bread, I almost passed out. Not only was it about pork chops, but it was about pork chops cooked in milk!

Now I have to laugh because the recipe is for a sugary-sweet, French-toast style bread that is fried in the shape of a pork chop, and even coated with tomato jam on top like a sauce coating. The whole unusual recipe and name lead me to believe it was passed down through the generations and could have been made to look like a casserole of pork chops with sauce. This would have fended off those trying to catch the new converts to Christianity who were hauled off to an Inquisition prison for not eating pork. This is the best look-alike to a pork chop that I have ever seen.

When I saw this recipe, I knew that my friend Cristina Lea Fernandes was the perfect one to try this. She is from Brazil, comes from a Converso background, and loves all the history of the Crypto-Jews. She has become very active in her synagogue, and I knew she would be the one to really get into the history surrounding this recipe. So, without further ado, here goes with this unusual recipe.

Two loaves of thick, country-grain bread (not sourdough, as the flavor overwhelms this recipe)

2 cups milk
¼ cup sugar
4 eggs, lightly beaten
¼ cup flour, approximately

Olive oil for frying
Tomato jelly
Several strips of sweet pimento

Reserve some crust from the bread. Mix the milk and sugar and wet the 2 loaves in this mixture until you can form a thick paste with your hands. Add the eggs and mix well. Add a little flour until the mixture is workable with and moldable in your hands.

Mold the mixture into the shape of a pork chop and fry in olive oil until golden brown, turning once on each side.

Cut the reserved crust into small sticks and fry until golden brown. Pierce the fritter with the crust sticks to look like a pork chop bone. Place in a casserole dish and cover with tomato jelly. Decorate with strips of sweet pimento.

Churros

Description: A fried delicacy made to be dipped in hot coffee or chocolate
Level: Difficult
Kosher: Pareve

The different grandmothers modified recipes many times, and I wanted to stay true to our history. I have two different types of churro. I always thought that this was a Cuban recipe, to be eaten with café con leche or hot chocolate, but the first time I traveled to Spain and saw the "churro" stand at the airport, I realized that all of these recipes of the new world dated back to the homeland of Spain. In Miami, these churros are sold at every street corner in Little Havana. They can be made into snakes as mentioned, but usually are made with something similar to a cookie press that makes the churros look like snakes with long lines or wedges. This is a true Spanish and Cuban recipe. When I made it, I used Recipe 1 and did not modify it. I was proud to know that I was embracing five-hundred-plus years of ancestry.

Recipe 1
3 cups water
1 teaspoon salt
3 cups all-purpose flour

Olive oil for frying
Granulated sugar for dusting the
    finished churro

Boil the water with the salt and slowly add the flour. Remove from heat and continue mixing by hand until blended well. Form into long snakes and deep-fry until golden brown. Drain and dust with sugar.

Recipe 2
1 cup water
3 heaping tablespoons flour
1 cup anise liqueur

Olive oil for frying
Granulated sugar for dusting the
    finished churro

Boil the water until it comes to a rolling boil and add the flour, mixing well. Let cool a little bit and then add the anise, again mixing well into the mixture. Form into long snakes with the churro press and deep-fry until golden brown. Drain and dust with sugar.

Cocadas

Description: A sweet coconut delicacy
Level: Difficult
Kosher: Pareve
Passover: Yes

When my great-grandmother left Spain and moved to Cuba, large parts of the family stayed behind. For many years I thought I had a random family member or two still in Spain, but I had no idea that I had a huge family still living in Zamora as well as in Oviedo in Spain. Only after I researched my genealogy did I reach out and meet these "new" family members. Many had been in touch with my grandparents for many years and yet others were new to the whole family. One of the aunts, named Angelita, had sent my grandmother several recipes in the early 1900s, and this is one of them.

I really have to thank my girlfriend Nilza for her incredible efforts in making these cocadas. Nilza was born in Brazil and had made a coconut ball recipe for me years before I approached her with this challenge, so I thought this recipe would be easy-peasy for her. That would have been true except that she had to make it again and again to get the ingredients and consistency correct. Nilza is a physician, so at the end of the process, I knew she took this on with surgical precision and the recipe would be perfect! At last count, she had to make these cocadas six times! She cut the sugar way down and played around with frozen coconut, fresh coconut, and dried coconut. She feels the fresh coconut was the best. The results are below. Nilza brought these to the grandmothers' Shabbat dinner, and they were loved by all! Thank you, Nilza, for not giving up!

Fresh Coconut Version

8 ounces fresh coconut

6 ounces sugar, finely ground in food processor (Nilza used the flat blade)

2 large eggs, lightly beaten

4 ounces dried and shredded coconut

Mix all ingredients well. Make balls of the mixture with wet hands and a tablespoon measuring spoon, and place them on a cookie sheet lined with parchment paper. Bake at 350°F for 15 minutes. Start watching them after 12 minutes to make sure they don't burn.

Frozen Shredded Coconut Version

14 ounces frozen shredded coconut, pulsed in food processor until finely shredded

4 ounces dried coconut flakes

6 ounces sugar, pulsed in food processor until fine

2 large eggs, lightly beaten

Mix all ingredients well. Form small balls with your hands, place them on a cookie sheet lined with parchment paper, and bake at 350°F for 12 to 15 minutes. Watch them carefully so they don't burn.

Coconut Sweets in Syrup

Description: A sweet coconut ball in a sugary syrup
Level: Medium
Kosher: Dairy

This recipe originates in Costa Rica and was passed down from my grandmother Mati. She used to tell me that these were a favorite in her household. When she grew up in Costa Rica, she used to make them with the lemon or orange flavor, and once she moved to Cuba she used rum, as it was so rampant on the island. My friend Kim Wolfenzon tried this out in her kitchen and made them both ways. Her family loved them both, and the dish was yummy! I appreciated that Kim sent me a highly detailed report with pictures, comments, and notes. Thanks to Kim, the recipe was modified for modern measurements.

The Sweets
2 large eggs
2 to 4 tablespoons sugar, depending
    on desired sweetness
1 cup milk
4 tablespoons butter, melted
1 teaspoon baking soda (bicarbonate)

3½ cups all-purpose flour
    (approximately — enough to form
    a paste that is not too hard)
Canola or coconut oil for frying
Coconut flakes

Beat the eggs with the sugar and then add the milk, butter, baking soda, and finally the flour. Roll out the dough (the thinner the better, to fry up quick) and form little 3-inch sticks. Roll these up and pan-fry in oil. Coat with coconut flakes and drizzle almibar (see recipe below) over them.

Almibar
2 cups water
1 cup sugar

1 tablespoon rum or other liqueur, or orange or lemon zest

Mix all together over medium-high heat, stirring constantly until a heavy syrup is formed.

Coat the pastries with coconut flakes and drizzle over them almibar in citrus or liqueur flavor – your choice!

Cake de Una Libra

Description: Pound cake
Level: Difficult
Kosher: Dairy

The title of this literally means Cake of One Pound, which leads me to believe this was the origin of the term "pound cake." I tackled this recipe myself even though I am not a sweets lover because, to be honest, none of my friends wanted to make such a rich cake loaded with sugar! The measurements are exactly the same as the grandmothers had written down in Spain, and the only difference with the instructions is that I did not separately beat and whip up the eggs. I whisked the eggs, then added the melted butter, sugar, milk, and vanilla. I mixed it all by hand vigorously for 3 to 4 minutes. The result is a delicious, thick, and dense pound cake. I think the original recipe should be followed because perhaps it would have been light and fluffy had I followed the initial instructions! This is a must-make cake!

8 medium eggs
1 pound butter
1 pound sugar

1 teaspoon vanilla extract
1 pound flour
½ cup whole milk

Separate the yolks from the egg whites. Beat the butter together with the sugar until the sugar is fully dissolved. Lightly beat the egg yolks and set aside. Beat the egg whites until snowy. Add the egg yolks to the butter-sugar mixture and then slowly add the egg whites and vanilla. Add the flour and milk and mix until creamy and well blended. Pour into a greased mold and bake at 350°F for 35 to 45 minutes or until golden brown. (In a Bundt pan, it took close to 55 minutes for the inserted knife to come out clean.)

Cream or Frosting for Pastry

Description: A unique frosting for cakes and pastries
Level: Medium
Kosher: Dairy
Passover: Depending on your tradition

This cream is to be used for frosting cakes, cupcakes, or cookies. It can also be used as cream for flaky pastry. What was interesting about this recipe in the book is that it used the measurement *cuartillo* for the milk. It is a very old unit of measure that goes hand in hand with the liter. One cuartillo is ½ liter, and ½ liter is 16 ounces or two cups. It also used the word *lumbre* for fire or stove. I found myself having the challenge of looking up many words to be able to bring it up to date. I am still amazed that I have recipes that are so old that the meanings of words have to be looked up!

6 egg yolks
2 egg whites
2 cups milk

7 tablespoons sugar
1 teaspoon cornstarch
Zest of two lemons

All the ingredients should be mixed together carefully until fully homogenized. Stir continuously on the stove at medium-high heat until the cream boils, and then lower heat and stir until it becomes hard and shiny. Take off the fire and mix for a few minutes. Pour into a cold metal mixing bowl and frost away or use as cream for flaky pastry.

Note: For a coffee-flavored frosting, eliminate the zest and add 6 ounces of liquid coffee, dissolving it into the milk before starting the other steps.

Dark Fruit Cake

Description: A rich and dark fruit cake
Level: Difficult
Kosher: Pareve

I waited until the day before Rosh Hashanah to make this recipe myself, as I felt that with all the dark, rich fruits and honey it was the perfect one for the New Year holiday, and I was right! I was rushed because there was so much cooking to do but it was worth it once I got this cake into the oven! In my whole life I have never had my house full of these most amazing and spicy aromatic scents! The cake itself is rich but not overpowering, and I drizzled dark honey all over it. A keeper for the holidays for sure! I have already included my modifications in the recipe below. Enjoy!

2 cups flour
2 teaspoons allspice
2 teaspoons cinnamon
½ teaspoon nutmeg
½ teaspoon clove powder
1 cup turbinado sugar, divided
    into 2
½ cup margarine
3 large eggs, separated
¼ cup dark honey

1 cup dark raisins
1½ pounds other dried fruits, cut
    up small (apricots, figs, cherries,
    dates, and other fruits may be
    used; I did not use candied fruit
    as I felt it might be too sweet)
¼ cup grape juice
½ teaspoon baking soda
    (bicarbonate)
1 tablespoon hot water

Mix together and sift the flour, allspice, cinnamon, nutmeg, and clove powder 3 times. Beat ½ cup sugar and the margarine together, making sure it is creamy. Beat the egg yolks with the other ½ cup sugar and add the honey. Mix the egg yolk mixture with the sugar and margarine mixture. Lightly beat the egg whites and fold in.

Add 1¾ cups of the flour-spice mix slowly until well mixed. Toss the dried fruits in the remaining flour-spice mix, and add to the mixture. Add the grape juice. Dissolve the baking soda in hot water and add to the mixture. Grease a large (9 x 11-inch), deep, Pyrex baking dish (like a lasagna dish) and cover the bottom with greased parchment paper. Put mixture into the dish and bake at 300°F for 1¼ hours. Check often for doneness. Remove from oven and drizzle dark honey over the top with a little bit of liqueur if desired.

Dulces en Almibar

Description: Sweets in syrup
Level: Medium
Kosher: Dairy

My friend Teri Perez has been researching her own family history for a long time. I met her early on during this quest and she has been able to reach the 1500s in the Galician area of Spain. Teri has not given up on finding out her real roots and works on this tirelessly. I have had the pleasure of sitting with her in my home for long periods of time and trying to unravel the web of Teri's family. We *will* get to the bottom of it one day, and the last time I spoke to her she was getting close. It was a treat to have Teri and her son at my home for her first Passover. He was the most inquisitive person at our table and had many questions for everyone! Teri was also one of the first to offer to make a recipe, and engaged her daughter Kristina Perez and friend Kelsey Harlow in the project. They made these delicious sweets and used the orange instead of the lemon zest. A highly recommended recipe!

I notice that many of the recipes of the grandmothers from Spain are made using a basic syrup known in Spanish as almibar. It is used as a base and as a liquid sugary coating as well. I also see that it varies from recipe to recipe. I have not tried to standardize the almibar, as I feel that each grandmother was doing her "own thing," and I did not want to disturb the authenticity of the recipes.

The Sweets

3 eggs, lightly beaten
6 heaping tablespoons sugar
6 heaping tablespoons butter, melted
1 teaspoon baking powder

½ pound flour, plus a bit more if necessary
¼ cup whole milk
Olive oil

Mix the eggs, sugar, butter, baking powder, and some of the flour until you can just form a small ball. Add the milk and then add more flour little by little until you can form a paste. The mixture should be as soft as possible. Drop by tablespoons into a deep fryer of oil, and after draining, put in a dish and pour the syrup over them.

Yet another Spanish delicacy!

Almibar

2 cups water

1 cup sugar

1 tablespoon rum or other liqueur

1 tablespoon orange or lemon zest

Mix all together over medium-high heat, stirring constantly, until a heavy syrup is formed.

Empanadas Mati

Description: Light and fluffy pastries shaped like small turnovers
Level: Medium
Kosher: Dairy

This recipe is from my maternal grandmother, whose name was Dora (I called her Mati). She is the one that I remember the most and especially when I make this recipe. She used to make these all the time and not only did I love them, so did everyone else in the family. I used to make them frequently from the time I started cooking at the age of 12 or so. I always made them using the recipe that I had memorized, because, in the back of my mind, I could always call her if I forgot. On the day she died, I was 19 years old, and even while saddened to the core, on the way to the funeral home, I finally wrote the recipe down. I will always remember her gentle and humble ways. I made these recently and took them to a friend's house for a break-fast, and they were snatched up faster than the bagels! The actual hand mixing of this recipe and baking brought me very close to the wonderful memories of baking with my grandmother.

1 pound butter, softened
2 large (8-ounce) packages
   cream cheese
2 pounds all-purpose flour
4 teaspoons baking powder
10 heaping tablespoons sugar

Fillings: could be guava, guava and
   cheese, or a mixture of tuna,
   olives, and raisins. (I always
   make them with guava.)
2 eggs, lightly beaten, for egg wash

Mix the butter and cream cheese together and then add the flour, baking powder, and sugar. Mix by hand until well blended. Put in refrigerator for 2 hours. Roll out on a floured surface and cut out circles that are 2 or 3 inches in diameter. Put a small piece of guava or other filling in the center of each circle and fold over to make a half moon. Press the sides together with a fork and make fork marks all around the empanada. Brush lightly with egg wash.

Place on a very well-greased cookie sheet, preferably aluminum, and bake at 350°F for 20 minutes. They will bake fully but never get dark golden brown, because of the large amounts of butter and cream cheese. Eat when cooled off, because filling could be very hot.

Crystallized Fruit

Description: Dried and sweetened fruit slices
Level: Easy
Kosher: Pareve
Passover: Yes

These fruits were made often by both sides of my family. I used to eat the sugared figs that my grandmother Mati would bring us from Costa Rica, where she was born, and a few times when she made them at home. My mom also made these many times when I was young. Her favorite was always the dried and crystallized orange slices. This is a very decorative and fun way to eat fruit (with a lot of sugar!). Children enjoy helping out in this but have little patience to wait the two days for the drying.

2 cups sugar
1 cup water
Assorted fruits: plums, cherries, peaches, pears, and figs, cut up or whole
Granulated sugar for sprinkling

Bring the sugar and water to a boil and add the fruits. Cook over a low heat until the fruit is softened. Take off the fire and set aside for two days.

Strain out the liquid and lay out the fruit on a tray until it is dry to the touch. Powder with granulated sugar and finish drying completely in a moderate oven or in the sun like the grandmothers used to.

Frituras

Description: A sugar-coated fried pastry
Level: Medium
Kosher: Dairy, modifiable to pareve

I asked my good friend Jackie Abels to make this one because many of the recipes for the grandmothers' desserts were fried and I knew that Jackie rarely fries anything. I wanted to be sure that even a non-fryer could make this recipe work and she did! The only change she made was to use coconut milk instead of regular milk so the recipe could be pareve. She added canola oil as a substitute for the olive oil because olive oil burns too quickly. Jackie brought these to the grandmothers' Shabbat dinner and she was sure that the fritters had burned, but in reality, we ate these with great gusto as they were just the right consistency with the perfect sweetness. Jackie dusted them with powdered sugar and they were yummy! So you see, Jackie Abels, even when you thought something did not work out correctly, it actually was great!

5 tablespoons all-purpose flour
5 tablespoons sugar
1 egg

2 tablespoons milk or coconut milk
2 teaspoons baking powder
Olive oil or canola oil for frying

Mix all ingredients well and drop into hot oil by the spoonful. Fry until golden brown and sprinkle with confectioners' sugar or honey if desired.

Galleticas

Description: A wonderful cookie recipe
Level: Easy
Kosher: Dairy

I found this very faded recipe written by my paternal grandmother, Mati. She was born and lived in Costa Rica all her life until she got married and moved to Cuba. On the recipe she wrote that these cookies were my dad's favorite as a child. I made them for him as soon as I found the recipe and the look on his face was unreal. It is incredible how recipes can evoke memories and long-forgotten images. Thank you, Mati, for reaching out to me through the decades and letting me put that dreamy smile on my dad's face again. As always, grandmothers save the day! Even though I had made it several times in Miami, I wanted another test baker, so I asked my colleague and author friend Corinne Brown to make them for me. Corinne has written several books on the Crypto-Jews of the Southwest and is the editor and publisher of the magazine of the Society for Crypto-Judaic Studies, *HaLapid*. She was so excited because she told me they tasted very Iberian to her! She also told me that the dough is very soft and when they bake, they puff up and never fully brown. Her family loved them with ice cream and berries, or just plain with a cup of coffee! Some of her recommendations are incorporated into the recipe below. She baked them for 14 minutes and they never browned, but Corinne lives at an altitude of 5,000 feet above sea level, so keep an eye on them. Enjoy!

2 cups all-purpose flour
½ teaspoon baking powder
¼ teaspoon salt
¾ cup white sugar
¼ cup salted butter

4 large eggs
½ teaspoon vanilla
½ teaspoon lemon juice
2 tablespoons whole milk

Mix together the flour, baking powder, salt, and sugar. Mix the butter, eggs, vanilla, lemon, and milk in a blender. Add to the dry ingredients and mix gently. Drop by teaspoonfuls onto a greased cookie sheet and bake at 350°F for 15 minutes or until golden brown.

Huevos Moles

Description: A thick, sweet pudding from the Canary Islands
Level: Easy
Kosher: Pareve
Passover: Yes

This is a recipe from the Canary Islands. I am not sure which grandmother finally wrote this one down but as far as I know it is only made in the Canary Islands. When I traced my dad's lineage, it led straight back to the Canary Islands, so I imagine it came from my dad's great-grandmother. It can be used as a sauce over crunchy *merengue* or pound cake or even biscuits. It can also be poured into goblets, cooled, and eaten as a pudding. I gave over this challenge to my Argentinean girlfriend Liliana Benveniste. I thought about it a lot before giving it to her because Lili is always so super busy that I felt bad bothering her with my project, but as busy as she is, she is also incredibly sweet and offered right away to participate. Liliana works tirelessly on behalf of the Sephardim, and she and her husband, Marcelo, own the largest online Sephardic magazine (www. esefarad.com). She is a famous, world-renowned Sephardic singer, and also is a champion of the preservation of the Ladino language, as well as a teacher of Ladino. Lili made this recipe exactly as the grandmothers had passed it down and she said it was very tasty! She made it straight and poured it into beautiful goblets. *Gracias, mi amiga!*

4 cups sugar
¹/3 cup water
1 cinnamon stick

3 medium-sized egg yolks, lightly
     beaten

Mix sugar, water, and cinnamon together over high heat, stirring constantly until it forms a thick syrup. While warm, slowly stir in the egg yolks until well blended. If desired, pour over a cake while the mixture is still warm, or pour into goblets and cool in refrigerator for 2 hours, then eat as a pudding.

Magdalenas

Description: A variation on madeleine cakes
Difficulty: Medium
Kosher: Dairy

This recipe was passed down to me by my paternal grandmother, Mati. Although she was born in Costa Rica, she descends from a French lineage that I found going back to the early 1700s. This recipe carries a legend that the cakes were originally made and named in the kitchens of Louis XV to honor a family cook by the name of Madeleine. They were first made in Lorraine, France, in 1755. I asked my daughter-in-law, Liana Vega Hernandez, to make these magdalenas. She was also born in Costa Rica and I felt it would honor my grandmother to have her make them. In English, they are known as madeleine cookies. Liana followed the recipe exactly and she even purchased a metal pan in the typical shell shape of the cookie. Liana told me that olive oil is just too heavy a flavor for this so she would highly recommend using a healthier and less sharp oil, such as avocado. She also told me that she cut the recipe in half and it worked out perfectly. She cautions strongly to keep a close eye on them, because they burn very easily in the shallow metal pan. Thank you, Liana. You made my grandmother proud, I'm sure!

10 eggs
1¼ pounds sugar
1¼ pounds flour

2¼ cups olive oil (Liana recommends a lighter-flavored oil)
Zest of 1 lemon

Separate the eggs and beat the egg whites until they are snowy and have peaks. Add the egg yolks and continue beating. Add the sugar until well mixed, and then the flour, and finally the oil, to which you have added some lemon zest. Mix all together and pour into cupcake paper molds or preferably a special shell-shaped madeleine cookie pan. Bake in a 350°F oven for 25 minutes or until a knife inserted in the center comes out clean. Given the caution that Liana mentions, perhaps a 300°F oven would be better, or start checking at 18 to 19 minutes.

Mantecaditos

Description: A melt-in-your-mouth cookie recipe
Level: Medium
Kosher: Pareve

The original recipes were made with lard in Spain but my grandmothers had already switched to vegetable shortening decades ago.

Colleague and fellow author Marcia Fine took on this recipe with her husband, Skip Feinstein. Marcia has been writing about Crypto-Jews and she has quite a following. They had to work with the recipe a lot to get it fine-tuned and delicious. It seems these cookies are addictive, so watch out! Here is what they said:

"The Great Cookie Experiment is complete! We made the first batch of mantecaditos and they fell apart. Skip's the chef around here so he made another batch using the whole egg and not just the yolk, plus a little water to moisten the mixture. I contributed by adding some chopped pecans (could be any nuts; I love nuts!). They came out great and delicious! Skip says they're addictive. They're best when they've cooled and are soft and chewy, but eating them this morning when they've firmed up hasn't discouraged us. Simple recipe and probably a standard. I can see making a thumb impression and putting a bit of raspberry jam there."

Thanks, Marcia and Skip! Marcia's literary expression shows through even when she writes about baking!

2 cups sugar
2½ cups flour
1 teaspoon salt
1 teaspoon baking powder

1 egg yolk, plus a little bit of water,
    to moisten the mixture
1 cup vegetable shortening

Mix together the sugar with the flour, salt, and baking powder. Then add the egg yolk and shortening. Make round cookies in your hand and place on a greased cookie sheet. Bake at 350°F for 10 minutes. Watch them closely so they don't burn. Cook until browned.

Orejuelas y Pestiños (1)

Description: Fried dough folded over, similar to hamantashen in shape
Level: Medium
Kosher: Pareve

These recipes are very typical ones of the region where my family lived for 500 years. Fermoselle, Spain, is on the banks of the Duero River and is known for its fine wines. These desserts were eaten all over Castille and their origin dates back to before 1492. While all the three cultures made these fried delicacies, the Moors, Jews, and Christians all used different toppings. What was most interesting to me about this recipe was that I found it written many, many times in all sorts of handwritings and on all types of paper. That tells me that different grandmothers wrote it down and at different times in history. I must have seen this particular one ten times. What is also interesting is that orejeula means ear, and we have an Ashkenazic equivalent for the holiday of Purim which is known as hamantashen, and this is also ear shaped. Purim became a very special holiday for the Crypto-Jews, and they even started praying to Esther and calling her St. Esther to disguise the fact that they were Jews. There is no evidence that points to this "ear" recipe being the same, but it is sure a coincidence! The following recipe was given to Jennifer Resnick, an accomplished cook who was born in South Africa, and I was grateful that someone with her experience was able to make comments on it. She told me that they tasted very good but dense, and is not sure if they were supposed to be fluffier. She said they turned out crisp on the outside and tender inside. She also told me that she used all the ingredients the grandmothers listed but did not get a consistency she could work with until she had used 6 + cups of flour, and even then, it was quite sticky. She used bamboo mats as the cooling rack after they were fried. She liked the anise flavor in the dough but would use a more fragrant honey the next time. Because she had to use so much more flour than the recipe calls for, perhaps using less wine would work as well. Thanks, Jen!

Dough

2 cups white wine

1 cup olive oil (½ for the dough, ½ for frying)

1 cup anise liqueur

1 cup finely ground flour

Honey Coating

1 cup honey

½ cup water

Mix all ingredients for the dough well and let sit covered for 5 hours. Take a piece of the mixture and extend over a bamboo mat or other drainable surface so as to let the oil flow off. Cut and fold like a tube, and fry in oil that is not too hot, letting them brown little by little. Let cool.

Slowly mix the honey coating ingredients over a medium-high heat, stirring constantly until it thickens. Pour over pastry.

Orejuelas y Pestiños (2)

Description: Fried dough folded over in envelope or figure-eight shapes
Level: Medium
Kosher: Pareve

This one is very similar to the pestiños and has almost the same ingredients. Whenever I found them in the grandmothers' writings it would always be orejuelas and pestiños, so given the similar ingredients perhaps they were made at the same times and for the same holiday. The big difference seems to be in the shape, and one using a honey coating and the other an almibar syrup.

Dough
1¼ cups flour
1 cup olive oil (1/2 for the dough, ½ for frying)

1 cup white wine

Place the flour in a mixing bowl and make an indentation in the center. Add the oil and white wine and mix by hand. Lay out on floured surface and make long strips with a roller. The strips should be about 10 to 12 inches long and about 1¼ inches wide. Fold the strips over like an envelope and fry in deep, hot oil.

You can also form into figure eights and fry, turning once until browned on both sides. Serve with almibar or honey on top.

Almibar

2 cups water

1 cup sugar

1 tablespoon rum or other liqueur

1 tablespoon orange or lemon zest

Mix all ingredients together over medium-high heat, stirring constantly, until a heavy syrup is formed.

Palitos del Cielo Tia Paulita

Description: A great biscuit for spreads or gravy
Level: Difficult
Kosher: Pareve

Tia Paulita was my great-great-aunt, who lived in Madrid in the 1800s. I have many pictures of her as a tall, elegant woman, always wearing a fur around her neck with very elegant and stately clothing. She never married but must have been an incredible cook because many of the recipes carried down are hers. My friend Marge Prenner, who lives in Miami, attempted this one and all I can say is that it just did not work out! She told me she started with 2 eggs instead of 3, and after 2½ cups of flour, the dough was super sticky. Not wanting to give up on Great-Great-Aunt Paulita, I tried again, but made it pareve instead of dairy, not thinking it would make a difference but it actually did. I tweaked the measurements below and all I can say is that even though this was intended to be a sweet recipe, I can see it being a great biscuit to use with gravy, or a fried dough like you can get at a carnival. It doesn't have a lot of flavor and needs something poured over it or sprinkled on top. And by the way, sticky dough that you throw into the hot oil is exactly what this is. An interesting recipe. Thanks, Marge, for giving me the basis to get this done in a different way.

3 medium eggs
4 tablespoons sugar (I would use ½
   cup if you want them sweet)
1 cup milk (I used almond milk)
4 tablespoons butter or margarine
Flour — enough to make a paste that
is not too hard (I used 1½ cups)
1 teaspoon baking powder
Shredded coconut or powdered sugar
   for coating
Oil for pan-frying

Beat the eggs with the sugar, add the milk and then the butter, and mix all well. Slowly start adding flour until you can form a paste that is not too hard. Add the baking powder. Shape into little bars and pan-fry until browned. When done, coat in shredded coconut or sprinkle with powdered sugar. Or, drizzle honey over them!

Pan-Fried Rosquitas

Description: A delicious pastry for coffee
Level: Medium
Kosher: Pareve

My colleague and friend Dr. Judith Cohen is an ethnomusicologist and professor who just happens to be the world's leading expert on medieval and Judeo-Spanish music. She specializes in bringing our musical legacy out of the woodwork, and, as a performer, many times utilizes the antique instruments of bygone days in her music. She made this recipe while staying in Mallorca with her friend Esperanza Bonet, who was born and raised in Ibiza and had learned how to make these as a small child, from her own ancestors. Palma de Mallorca is home to the Chuetas, as the Crypto-Jews of the island became known. This is one of the original Chueta recipes. After they made the rosquitas (in Malorca they call them rosquillas), they sat down to enjoy them dipped into a cup of café con leche! Thank you so much, Judith and Esperanza!

6 tablespoons sugar
6 medium eggs, separated
2 to 3 handfuls flour (medium-sized women's hands)

Sunflower oil for frying
Bread crumbs from the store or from leftover bread

Add the sugar to the egg yolks and mix well by hand. Add the flour bit by bit, adding more if necessary for a texture that will allow you to pick it up and move it as one piece. Add the flour slowly so as not to use more than required. The dough should not be sticky.

Put a light coating of flour on the table or whatever surface is being used, to prevent sticking.

Roll out the dough and make several snakes about 6 inches long by ¼ inch wide. Form into circles or doughnut shapes.

Pour the oil into a frying pan and start heating the oil.

Prepare a plate with bread crumbs (store-bought ones will do, and we used them for this preparation, but in the grandmothers' time and still now, for many women, traditionally, they would be manually prepared from leftover bread).

Prepare another plate with slightly beaten egg whites. Dip the rosquitas in the bread crumbs and then in the eggs, then once again in the bread crumbs (important: in that order: crumbs, eggs, crumbs again). Fry until golden brown and enjoy.

Panatela

Description: Thick pound cake
Level: Medium
Kosher: Pareve

My colleague Kit Racette quickly offered to make a recipe. These days Kit lives in Canada and I am truly appreciative that she took on my project. She made it once and it came out like a Yorkshire pudding yet she persisted until it came out perfect. She modified the recipe and insists that readers know it is important that the eggs get folded in slowly! The end result was perfect. Kit, thank you not only for being a test baker but also for always being so encouraging about my work in regaining my ancestral memories. I really appreciate that she took the time to make this one several times and the final result is below with all her ingredient changes and techniques added in! Kit, you are the best!

Cake
6 eggs
Pinch of salt
½ cup sugar

1 cup all-purpose flour, sifted
1 teaspoon orange essence

Separate the egg whites from the yolks and beat the whites with the salt until they form peaks. Add the sugar little by little. Fold in the beaten egg yolks and then the flour and the essence. Put in a greased and floured square Pyrex pan and bake at 350°F until a knife inserted in the center comes out clean (about 30 minutes). Serve with wine almibar drizzled over the top.

Almibar de Vino to Drizzle on Top

⅔ cup sugar

4 tablespoons sweet red wine

4 tablespoons water

Mix slowly over medium-high heat until it becomes thick and syrupy. Set aside to pour over the panatela.

Rosquillas Dora

Description: Very similar to a cinnamon and sugar doughnut
Level: Medium
Kosher: Pareve

Dora is my paternal grandmother. We always called her Mati. She was one of the sweetest and gentlest people I have ever had the honor of knowing. She was born in Costa Rica from a French maternal lineage. I have traced her ancestry back to the late 1600s on her mother's side, and they were from a small village in France in the Bordeaux region that was known to have sheltered the Crypto-Jews after the expulsion. Unlike my maternal grandmother, I have not been able to prove they were Crypto-Jews but there is a lot of circumstantial evidence on that branch of the family as well. Interestingly enough I have found many DNA matches from the Jews of that region but no aha moment yet. This recipe had the measurements in eggshell sizes, and as I cooked this with my grandmother Mati, we slowly changed over to modern measurements. This recipe will be round like a small doughnut hole. I gave this recipe over to a friend and fellow Converso descendant Denise Febres Rodriguez and her daughter Nya. They had a great time making this recipe and did not have to change anything! They made it right before Yom Kippur so that it would be waiting for them after the fast! Thank you, Denise and Nya, for making this a mother-daughter project!

3 eggs
1 teaspoon baking powder
4 tablespoons sugar
6 tablespoons olive oil

1 cup or less all-purpose flour
Extra olive oil, for frying
Granulated sugar, for coating
Cinnamon, for coating (optional)

Mix eggs, baking powder, sugar, and olive oil together. Add flour until you can make doughnut-hole shapes with your hands. The objective is to make the mix as soft as possible.

Drop the shapes into very hot oil and fry, lowering the heat as the oil becomes too hot, and turning them until golden brown. Liberally coat with granulated sugar or with a granulated sugar and cinnamon mixture. Drain on paper towels.

Merengue Royal

Description: A fluffy and versatile meringue recipe
Level: Easy
Kosher: Pareve
Passover: Yes

The very first thing I ever cooked with both of my grandmothers was *merengue*. I still recall being at the home of one or the other and each making it her own way. One used to tell me that if I didn't add a tiny bit of vinegar it would not work and the other would say that I needed to add a pinch of cream of tartar. Through the years, I combined the recipes of both the grandmothers, and the recipe below is the best one yet. This became a staple in my home for Passover and there is not a year that I don't have this on my dessert table.

I usually prefer mine white but have made them in pastel colors for showers and other "ladies'" events.

¾ cup egg whites
2 cups sugar
1½ teaspoons vinegar, or a pinch of
    cream of tartar

Food coloring (optional)

Beat the egg whites (adding a tiny bit of food coloring if you wish) until you can barely make peaks. Add the sugar little by little while continuing to beat the mixture. Slowly add the vinegar in without stopping. Beat the mixture until you can make peaks that stand straight up.

Preheat the oven to 275°F. Grease a cookie sheet or cover with parchment paper. Scoop a tablespoon of the mixture and push it onto the cookie sheet with the help of another spoon. Bake for 40 minutes. They should be crunchy on the outside and semi-soft on the inside.

Royal Butter Cake

Description: A rich and dense cake
Level: Medium
Kosher: Dairy

My dear friend Cindy Lewin made this cake, and below is the recipe with her modifications. The original recipe called for 3 large eggs but since so many people told me that the batters were coming out very sticky, I modified to read 2 to 3 medium eggs instead. She told me it was deelish! She did say, though, that it should have some jam or another frosting, as by itself it might seem to some people to be a bit bland. She brought me over a slice and I thought it was deelish as well, with nothing added! Thanks, Cindy, for taking the time to help out in this important project of recuperating memories! This particular recipe was one that my grandmother used to make often and serve sliced at her canasta games. She always told me it was a "family recipe."

1¼ cups sugar
½ cup melted butter
2 to 3 medium eggs, separated
1 teaspoon vanilla extract

2¼ cups all-purpose flour
2½ teaspoons baking powder
½ teaspoon salt
⅔ cup milk

Add the sugar to the butter slowly and mix well until blended. Beat the yolks and add to the butter and sugar mixture. Mix until well blended. Add the vanilla and make sure all ingredients are well blended. Mix all the dry ingredients together, and little by little add to the butter mixture while incorporating the milk at the same time.

Beat the egg whites until they reach a snowy peak, and fold into the mixture. Bake at 350°F in a small square, greased pan for 45 minutes, testing often in the center to be sure it is done.

Sponge Cake

Description: A perfect sponge cake for Passover
Level: Medium
Kosher: Pareve
Passover: Modifiable

This recipe surprised me when I saw it because it contained a staple used on Passover: potato starch. I asked the rebbetzin of my community, Sima Becker, to tackle this one for me. She was very gracious and made it immediately. I was very appreciative, as she was already digging into the yearly ritual of cleaning for Passover, which literally turns a house upside-down. It is a version of spring cleaning on steroids! When I first converted, and way before I knew I had Jewish ancestry, my biggest struggle was with my old Spanish and Cuban foods. I did not understand the new and different cuts of meat, I had nowhere to go for guava pastries, and most of all, I had no idea how to adapt my old recipes to meet the kosher guidelines. It was Sima who patiently showed me different ways to get around this while teaching me new recipes. I will be forever grateful for those early days of teaching that allowed me to feel comfortable in my kitchen once again. Thank you, Sima, for finding kosher guava pastries for me that first year of my conversion. You didn't quite understand my craving but it made a world of difference to me!

18 yolks from large eggs
4 tablespoons flour or potato starch
2¼ tablespoons lime juice

4 cups water
3 cups sugar
1 cinnamon stick

Beat the yolks until fluffy. Mix in the flour. Place in a greased mold and bake at 275°F for 20 to 30 minutes. Take out of oven and cool on a baking rack.

Make a light syrup on the stove by combining the lime juice, water, sugar, and cinnamon. Heat until boiling and the syrup has become thicker but not too thick. Pierce cake all over with a fork and pour hot syrup over it until well absorbed.

Sima tells me that the secret is to whip the egg yolks until frothy so as to help the cake rise on its own. She also liked the fact that there was no sugar in the cake itself, so it could be as sweet as you wanted to make it with the syrup. She later became even more creative when she used the leftover egg whites: she beat them with sugar into a snow, folded them into frozen strawberries, and made a perfect Passover sorbet.

Sima also told me that this recipe, without the syrup, is a perfect one for Passover buns. She used the cake batter, added fried onions, and baked them in muffin tins. The consistency was dense enough to bake, split in half, and make sandwiches.

How creative is that? Thank you, Sima, for three recipes from one! (I wonder if the grandmothers did this also?)

Spanish Cake

Description: A light and fluffy cake
Level: Medium
Kosher: Dairy

Marcia Finkel, my genealogy buddy, offered right away to make a recipe. I was glad that it would be Marcia because she is the most methodical genealogist I know. She and I have often lectured together, and I was sure she would end up making a PowerPoint of this recipe! She told me that she loves to bake, so naturally I gave her a cake recipe! I was certain that if anyone could tweak a recipe, it would be Marcia. She made the cake and took it to the highest test tasters: the participants in her neighborhood mahjong game. Everyone loved it. She gave us a lot of great comments and tips. So glad you made this for us, Marcia. Thank you!

½ pound butter, melted
2 cups sugar
3 cups all-purpose flour
1 tablespoon baking powder

6 eggs
1 cup milk
1 tablespoon vanilla essence

In a large mixing bowl, cream together the butter and the sugar until well mixed and the sugar has almost dissolved. Add the flour little by little and mix in the baking powder. Beat the eggs and milk and vanilla together and add into the mixture. Pour into three separate (8-inch-round) lightly greased pans and bake at 350°F degree for 40 minutes.

Frost all three layers with your favorite frosting. Marcia does not usually frost her cakes, so instead of making homemade frosting, she purchased 2 containers of 15.5 ounces each of a rich and creamy chocolate chip frosting, and it gave the cake the added dimension. Thank you, Marcia, for going the extra mile.

Sugar Cookies

Description: An old-fashioned sugar cookie recipe
Level: Medium
Kosher: Dairy

As I have explained, this entire cookbook has been trial and error for the very ancient recipes of my grandmothers. Some of the recipes were so old that the paper could barely be read. For the most part, we have been lucky that they have worked out with major or minor tweaking, but in some cases they have not worked out at all. My colleague and longtime friend Adina Moryosef, from Netanya Academic College in Israel, took on what seemed to be a simple sugar cookie recipe, yet it did not work out at all. The mixture was too sticky no matter how much she tried. Adina works day in and day out with the descendants of Crypto-Jews and is always super busy. I truly appreciate that she tried, and I leave this recipe in here, intact from the grandmothers' writings, as a challenge to anyone who wishes to tackle it. If you can get this one to work, please send me an email and let me know what changes you made. I suspect that a cup of butter might be a bit much. Thank you so, so much, Adina. You gave it your all!

3 cups flour
1 teaspoon baking powder
1 teaspoon salt
1¼ cups sugar

3 small eggs
1 cup butter
1 teaspoon vanilla extract

Mix all the dry ingredients together. Add the unbeaten eggs first and then the butter and vanilla.

Mix all ingredients well. With a rolling pin, roll the mixture out as thin as possible and cut into round-shape cookies with the edge of a drinking glass. (I am sure you can use a cookie cutter, but keeping true to the authentic grandmothers' recipes, I always use a glass when I make their recipes.) Place on a greased cookie sheet. Preheat the oven to 350°F and bake for 8 minutes until golden brown.

Sweet Toasts

Description: A basic sweet, small cookie snack

Level: Medium

Kosher: Pareve

Passover: Depends on your tradition

It is always so difficult to find good recipes that can be used for Passover, yet this one can be used if you are of the Sephardic tradition and use corn products (which are considered *kitniyot* – see glossary) during Passover. The Ashkenazic tradition does not use corn products during this time. I am certain that my Sephardic family made this year after year, as the page in the hand-bound cookbook was well worn.

My good friend Helaine Weissman from Miami was the first one to not only volunteer to try a recipe, but the very first one to bake it, take pictures, and comment. I love what she wrote after making it, as she tried it out with her grandchildren while telling them the history of the Spanish Jews before the Inquisition. Here is what she told me: "I just finished making the sweet toasts, and I believe some of your grandmothers were with me while I baked. My grandson Leo walked in while the toasts were cooking, and he said my house 'smells like old people!!'"

Based on her experience, we have made some changes to the recipe. Here are her comments: "I used 6 extra-large eggs and I think the taste was too eggy. So maybe using fewer extra-large eggs, or 6 large eggs, would have been better. I baked them in a mini loaf pan for 20 minutes. After slicing I baked each side for 6 to 8 minutes. The recipe made about 30 pieces (depending on the thickness of your slices)." Thanks, Helaine. You are the best!

6 medium to large eggs, separated
1 cup sugar

1 cup cornstarch
1 tablespoon baking powder

Beat the egg whites until they form peaks. Add the egg yolks and beat for 10 minutes more. Slowly add the sugar, beat again thoroughly, and finally add the cornstarch and baking powder until well mixed. Pour into any small greased metal mold that can be baked, such as biscuit molds or small cornbread molds. Bake at 350°F for 20 minutes. Take out of molds, cool, and cut into small biscotti size. Put back in oven until golden brown on all sides, about 6 to 8 minutes.

Tocino del Cielo

Description: A pareve, denser version of flan
Level: Medium
Kosher: Pareve
Passover: Yes

This is literally translated as "bacon from heaven." I gave this recipe, copied from the grandmothers' papers, to my daughter, Nicole Hernandez. Even though Nicole was born in the States, she identifies strongly with the Cuban culture, and what could be more Cuban than tocino del cielo? This specialty is served at every single Cuban restaurant for dessert, and it is a staple in Miami. Tocino del cielo is a good alternative to flan or custard, which contain milk. It is a treat to have such a rich dessert be beautiful as well as tasty, pareve, and perfect for Passover. I was very surprised to learn it is known as a "Sephardic" recipe because I always thought it was from Cuba, but apparently it has been made by Sephardic Jews for centuries. Why am I not surprised? When my daughter tried to make this with the original measurements of the grandmothers, it was a total disaster. She said instead of a custard, it turned out like a crepe! None of these recipes as translated from the original were a slam dunk. In most cases the ingredients have been modified by the test cooks again and again. I then gave it a shot myself, tweaked the ingredients again quite a bit, and made it this Passover. It was not only beautiful, it was also delicious! I took out the whole egg and left the yolks only, and I also incorporated more boiling time for the almibar, as I felt the dessert needed to be denser. We have now tweaked this to perfection to be passed down to future generations.

2 cups water
2 cups sugar
12 egg yolks

1 piece natural vanilla bean, about
2 inches long, or 2 teaspoons
vanilla extract

Boil the water with 1 cup of sugar, stirring constantly, until it becomes a heavy syrup. Set aside and let cool. Slightly beat the egg yolks and add the syrup and the vanilla. (Make sure the syrup, or almibar as it is called, is completely cooled or you will cook the egg yolks!)

Melt one cup of sugar in a pan over medium-high heat until it becomes a light brown syrup. Quickly remove from the stove and pour into your mold or molds, making sure the bottom is covered as well as a little bit up the sides of the mold. When cool, set your molds into the refrigerator a few minutes until the candy crackles. You can use two 6-inch aluminum molds like I did or individual aluminum cupcake tins or even a cake mold.

Put the egg mixture into the molds and place them into a 275°F oven inside a large aluminum pan full of water. These molds must cook inside a water bath, and many times it is the actual water bath that is doing the gentle cooking of the dessert versus the oven. Make sure that not one drop of water falls into the molds or the whole thing will be ruined.

Bake between 45 minutes to 1 hour until a toothpick inserted comes out clean.

Wait until it is cold to unmold. I let it cool in the refrigerator overnight. Run a knife around the edge and turn upside down on your serving dish, and the caramel or almibar mixture will be on the top. Beautiful!

Sponge Rusk

Description: A round cake that is fragrant and layered with flavor
Level: Medium
Kosher: Pareve
Passover: Yes

As I have been reading recipes from many of the grandmothers and also from different times in history, sometimes I know exactly where they came from exactly, and other times, I am able to guess the origin of the recipe from the ingredients the grandmother used. This particular recipe is clearly marked Madrid, March 5, Thursday, 1936.

6 eggs, separated
1 cup sugar

1 cup potato starch
1 tablespoon baking powder

Beat the egg whites until they are almost at the snowy peak point of *merengue* and then add the yolks. Mix for another 10 minutes. Slowly add the sugar and then the potato starch and baking powder, and continue mixing until well blended.

Place the mixture in molds only until half full to give the opportunity for the rusk to rise. Bake at 350°F for 35 minutes, checking often to make sure it doesn't burn. A knife inserted in the center should come out clean. When browned, take out of molds, cool, and cut into 2-inch strips. Put back in oven to become golden brown on all sides. A truly delicious cake!

Torta de Manzana

Description: A light and buttery apple cake
Level: Difficult
Kosher: Dairy

This seemed like a straightforward recipe but I never imagined the crust to be the flakiest, best ever! My close friend Batya Goldman took this project head-on. Batya comes from a background very similar to mine, and the eerie thing is that we even look alike. We always tease that she is my long-lost sister. When I gave Batya this recipe, I had no idea that she was a secret baker at heart. I knew her for her excellence in the academic world, as a Reiki master, and for a myriad of other talents. Batya is an incredibly knowledgeable and versatile woman, and she is also super busy and took time out to make this recipe for this book. She knows that the recuperation of our lost memories is crucial to the Jewish people. Below is the recipe with her changes incorporated. Thank you so much, my friend.

¼ cup butter
¼ cup vegetable shortening
¼ cup cold water
2 cups all-purpose flour + 2 tablespoons

2 medium-size apples, cored and peeled
¾ cup sugar

Mix the butter, shortening, water, and flour but do not knead strongly. Divide the dough into two parts. Grate the apples and mix with the sugar. Roll out the dough and place half in a pie shell (8-inch rather than 9-inch). Put the apple mixture inside and cover with the rest of the dough. Seal up the sides with your fingers and poke holes on top with a fork. Bake at 350°F for 45 minutes or until golden brown.

Beverages

Chartreusse

Description: A historic Spanish beverage
Level: Difficult
Kosher: Pareve

As I turned the well-worn pages of the grandmothers' cookbooks, I didn't know what I was going to find. I was sure from the get-go that the experience would be enlightening but what I did not expect was to meet my grandmothers so many decades later via their recipes.

This recipe was in the book of my paternal grandmother, Mati, whose ancestry leads back to France. This recipe must have passed down through the generations, as it is a French liqueur that was known to have been made since 1737 by the Carthusian monks. The legend goes that a manuscript was given to them in 1605 by Francois d'Estrées, who had been born in 1573 and was later a diplomat and Marshal of France. It was known to have been made with over 130 herbs, plants, and flowers, and had a distinctive color. While this version is not as complex, it was interesting to find it in my grandmothers' recipes. I decided not to change the units of measure in this recipe and I give it to you in its original version. It is not one that I tried out or made, but I am putting it here for historical value.

½ liter wine alcohol
½ liter water
2 tablespoons vegetable elixir

½ kilo sugar
Pinch of saffron

Mix all ingredients together and boil for 20 minutes. Let sit overnight. Boil again the next day and let sit again, and then let the mixture rest for 3 to 4 days. Pass through filter paper and bottle. The liqueur ages in the bottle quite nicely.

Coctel Comodoro

Description: A Cuban cocktail, mixing rum with curaçao liqueur
Level: Easy
Kosher: Pareve

Imagine my surprise when I found handwritten by my dad, many years ago, all his cocktail recipes, hidden inside one of the books of the grandmothers. Since I don't have much knowledge of mixed drinks, I looked this one up in several books and found many different variations with totally different recipes. But this is the one that my dad had written down and was precious to him, so in honor of the grandfathers, I included some of my dad's favorite cocktails. I should add that in traditional Cuban households, it is usually the man who is in charge of making the cocktails or the punch, and in mine this was no exception. It was always my grandfather and then my dad, so all of the liqueur and cocktail recipes below belong to them.

1 ounce pineapple juice
1 ounce rum
3 drops marasquino (maraschino
    liqueur)

3 drops curaçao liqueur
Shake together with two ice cubes
    and serve.

Crème de Vie

Description: An eggnog-type drink
Level: Medium
Kosher: Pareve
Passover: Yes

In my family, this recipe was always made during the December holidays. Beautiful bottles were saved throughout the year, and the crème de vie was funneled in, and the bottles sealed and decorated with beautifully colored ribbon and given as gifts. Usually the elder women were making this for the younger ones and they always came to the family parties with armloads of bottles. This recipe was modified through the years as, initially, I can see in the worn cookbook that it was made with milk heated slowly for a long time with sugar. The newer generations of grandmothers changed over to condensed milk. Also, I see that originally, it used a cup full of anise liqueur, and in Cuba, where my great-grandmother and grandmother eventually lived, it was changed to rum, which was so popular in the small island nation.

2 cups sugar
1 cup water
1 small (10–12 oz.) can condensed
   milk

1 canful of rum (measure using
   empty condensed milk can)
1 squirt vanilla essence or vanilla
   liqueur
4 egg yolks

Dissolve the sugar completely in the water to make a syrup. Mix in the condensed milk, then the rum, vanilla, and egg yolks.

Mix well and funnel into beautiful bottles.

Mulata

Description: A rum and lemon cocktail
Level: Easy
Kosher: Pareve
Passover: Yes

This cocktail was one of my dad's favorites to serve guests because of how easy it was to make. No super-special ingredients were needed, and if someone popped into the house, he could serve this in a flash.

1 ounce lemon zest
1 teaspoon sugar

2 ounces rum
Add ice and mix.

Pineapple Punch

Description: A light party punch
Level: Easy
Kosher: Pareve

I have made this punch recipe many times for parties, with and without the rum, and I have also substituted a light, white, fizzy wine like Moscato. I have written out the recipe just as my dad had it, but I always used no more than a cup of sugar. The fizzy pineapple soda is the "secret ingredient" to this punch. Enjoy!

12 cans carbonated pineapple soda
2 bottles rum
Juice of 10 large oranges
Juice of 4 large grapefruit

4 pounds white sugar
½ bottle grenadine
Cool all the ingredients in the refrigerator overnight.

Ponche Cuba

Description: A hard cider beverage that packs a punch
Level: Easy
Kosher: Pareve
Passover: Yes

My dad had a small note written on this one that this was THE best of all the punch recipes. I never tried it as I was daunted by the sheer amount of ingredients. The recipe calls for bottlesful and gives no specific size. It is my experience that the bottles were small, as they were back in the day, so I would always use a smaller size when available versus a huge, 2-liter bottle of soda that is available these days. So here goes with the recipe and his last thoughts on this punch!

6½ bottles cider
6½ bottles seltzer
1 liter rum
½ bottle grenadine
4 grapefruits

3 cups sugar
4½ cups ginger ale
Juice of 2 lemons
Mix all together and add ice.

Simple Punch

Description: A cider punch with layers of flavor
Level: Medium
Kosher: Dairy or Pareve

This recipe used words and terminology that are only found in the Spanish of Costa Rica, where my paternal grandmother was from. Costa Rica, as well as Cuba, where she lived after she married my grandfather, are both known for excellent rum, so I am not sure if the recipe came down her family line that settled in Costa Rica in the 1700s or after moving to Cuba. In any event, this simple punch is not only simple but it's wonderful as well! I have written it out exactly like my great-grandmother did.

6½ cups hard cider (made from apples from North America)
6½ cups seltzer
4½ cups rum
16 ounces grenadine

3 pounds sugar
4½ cups ginger ale
1 quart dairy or pareve ice cream

Blend all ingredients in a large punch bowl and add the ice cream in scoops on top right before serving.

Epilogue

From start to finish, this was one incredible journey. The minute I found those tiny pieces of paper with all the recipes, I knew I was in for a ride that would be hard to get off till the very end. This was emotional on so many levels, starting with reading and touching the handwritings of the grandmothers I had been researching for decades, the incredible lift from my close friends and colleagues helping out with gladness in their hearts, and finally to actually cooking so many of these dishes in my own kitchen and wondering what was in the minds of the grandmothers when they cooked them decades or even hundreds of years ago. More than any other research I have done, this project took me to the edge of time, and I felt I had finally connected with them in a way I never felt would be possible. I miss my own grandmothers and other ancestors who have already left, yet this legacy that I held in my hands and that I now transmit to you is a rare and valuable jewel. I will always be grateful to my grandmothers, Maneni and Mati, for ensuring these left their countries, and for my mom, who kept all of these boxes intact for me. I love all of you who helped, who asked, who came forward with no prompting to help out. You are truly the best of friends. Thank you all for being a part of my life and for keeping before us the family history of my Crypto-Jewish family, who lost it all, then gained it all back a hundredfold.

Glossary

adafina. The Sephardic version of the stew made and eaten for the Sabbath. Jewish law forbids cooking on the Sabbath, so these large stews were traditionally made before the Sabbath and then kept warm. The grandmothers' version of *adafina,* cocido madrileño, is in this book.

almibar. A simple syrup used in many Spanish and Cuban recipes, consisting only of water boiled with sugar and some flavored essence.

Ashkenazic. Deriving from Jews whose ancestors came primarily from Europe, including countries such as Germany, France, Poland, Russia, Lithuania, and Hungary.

bikur cholim. This refers to the Jewish commandment of visiting the sick and extending a hand to those who are ill.

buñuelos. Loosely translated, a dessert made of fried dough. It may be round or have a particular shape.

café con leche. The typical Spanish and Cuban hot milk with coffee that is a staple in the home for breakfast.

chesed. An act of kindness and benevolence.

chiricaya. A flan- or custard-like dessert from the Cartago area of Costa Rica.

cholent. A typical Ashkenazic Jewish dish that starts cooking before the Sabbath and is kept hot, often in a slow cooker so that it can be eaten on the Sabbath. The Ashkenazic version usually will have chunks of beef, beans, potatoes, and barley. Every cook has his or her own recipe, and the taste varies from household to household.

Chueta. The Crypto-Jews in Spain and Portugal were called by many demeaning names, and on the Island of Mallorca they were called Chuetas, as in chuleta, which means pork chop or pig.

hafrashat challah. Literally, "separating challah." Taking a portion of challah (bread) dough and dedicating it. This is a biblical obligation specified in Numbers 15:17–21. This symbolic offering is made with a blessing still today in observant Jewish homes.

Juban. A term used widely in the United States for people who are Cuban and Jewish.

kitniyot. Corn, lentils, other types of legumes, and much more. These are foods that Jewish law allows Sephardic but not Ashkenazic Jews to eat on Passover.

kosher dietary laws. A set of rules and regulations that, among other restrictions, tells Jews what animals to eat, how they are to be slaughtered, and what foods should be eaten together or separately.

Mimouna. Some Sephardic Jews have a tradition to celebrate the end of Passover with a large party rich in desserts and symbolic fruits and foods. Usually, no meat will be eaten.

motza'ei Shabbat. This is the time after the end of Shabbat at nightfall on Saturday night.

pareve. A pareve food or ingredient is one that is neither dairy nor meat, for example, eggs, fruits, and vegetables. We make this distinction because the Jewish dietary laws do not allow dairy and meat to be mixed, but pareve foods can be eaten with either.

Passover. A Jewish holiday celebrating the Israelites' liberation from slavery in ancient Egypt, during which we do not use our regular flour products or eat anything leavened. We also take great pains to be certain that there are no products in the house that contain these ingredients. We eliminate our usual breads, cookies, pasta, etc.

Purim. A holiday that commemorates the saving of the Jewish people from the plot of their enemy Haman to annihilate them. On this holiday, there is a public reading of the Book of Esther and much merriment. Many communities dress in costumes and masks.

Raya. This is the area along the length of the Duero River (as it is known in Spain – Douro in Portugal). Crypto-Jews often lived in this area and went seamlessly from Spain to Portugal and back, just as my own family did.

rebbetzin. The wife of a rabbi who is usually a religious and spiritual leader in her own right.

Sephardim. Jews whose origins are from Spain. Because there were no Spanish Jews for centuries, these communities were more recently from the Ottoman Empire, North Africa, and Israel.

shawarma. A mixture of meat, turkey, chicken, or veal that is roasted and served in slices to be eaten usually inside a pita bread. Many cultures in the Middle East claim this dish as their own.

tzedakah. Literally, "justice." The Hebrew word for charity. It is a moral obligation in Judaism to give charity and be charitable.

Index